COMMUNICATION

in general education

BROWN

GENERAL EDUCATION SERIES

EARL J. MCGRATH, *General Editor, Institute of Higher Education, Teachers College, Columbia University*

CARPENTER: *The Larger Learning*

CARLIN: *Curriculum Building in General Education*

FISHER: *Humanities in General Education*

HAUN: *Science in General Education*

MAYHEW: *Social Science in General Education*

MORSE-DRESSEL: *General Education for Personal Maturity*

SHOEMAKER-FORSDALE: *Communication in General Education*

COMMUNICATION
in general education

College Composition and Communication

FRANCIS SHOEMAKER and LOUIS FORSDALE
Editors

13002

Wm. C. Brown Company Publishers, *Dubuque, Iowa*

Manufactured by WM. C. BROWN CO. INC., Dubuque, Iowa

Printed in U. S. A.

table of contents

foreword

In 1949 a series of four volumes published by the Wm. C. Brown Company Publishers reviewed various general education programs in the major divisions of knowledge. Among these publications, one entitled *Communication in General Education* contained descriptions of a wide variety of courses in colleges and universities designed to acquaint the student with the character of his own language and to cultivate basic skills in its usage.

In the past decade the whole field of communication has undergone rapid and in some institutions fundamental change. Many colleges and universities have introduced new concepts concerning the nature of communication, devised new systems for making it more effective, and inaugurated new systems for teaching this subject as a part of the general education of American youth. The present volume reviews many of the important changes that have occurred in recent years in the teaching of communication skills and the related intellectual processes.

Francis Shoemaker and Louis Forsdale have studied and written about communication for a period of years. Both have also taught this subject at the undergraduate and the graduate level. They are familiar with developments throughout the United States in the college curriculum. In this volume they have brought together descriptions of some of the courses in institutions included in the earlier volumes on the same subject issued more than a decade ago, and they have also added others from persons and institutions not represented in that volume.

Those working in the other divisions of knowledge will be interested in the companion volumes also issued by the William C. Brown Company Publishers. They are: Science in General Education, Social Sciences in General Education, Curriculum Building in General Education, General Education for Personal Maturity, Humanities in General Education, and the Larger Learning.

Earl J. McGrath
Executive Officer
Institute of Higher Education

editors' preface

Several months ago, while this volume was in its initial planning stage, one of us met a mathematical-physicist from Johns Hopkins — seat mate on a flight from Washington to Nashville. Conversation moved quickly to climate — the intellectual climate of near-saturation with new knowledge available beyond the present limits of general comprehension in the culture — and the resulting phenomenon of increased rate of change and the problem of instituting appropriate design and selectivity in education to help young people to participate earlier in the direction of this change. J. R. Cominsky's comment in The Saturday Review seemed pertinent: "Today, any education is virtually obsolete in ten years." The mathematical-physicist shook his head. "That isn't so in my field. In my field it is two months!"

This conversation, juxtaposed with some academic spokesmanship and some public inquiry and advocacy of return to the "three R's," symbolizes dramatically part of the context in which this book comes into being. It is purely coincidental that Cominsky's ten years should equal the span since Earl J. McGrath's pioneer book[1] as part of a series on General Education in 1949. But in our correspondence with departmental chairmen and course directors, inviting their descriptive accounts of current freshman courses, we were clearly conscious of increasing pressure for course evolution when we asked: ". . . . in the light of new technology, changing student population and new scholarship in our field, what do you think your course will look like in 1970?" The recency of thorough course revision on many campuses and the awareness of constant incremental revision led most spokesmen to feel that present course patterns, essentially unchanged, would be appropriate for the next ten years.

---

[1]McGrath, Earl J. (Ed.) *Communication in General Education.* Dubuque: W. C. Brown, 1949.

Introducing this volume with this positional emphasis on change may seem odd, when our major concern is to provide a documentary overview of college freshman instruction in courses titled English, Composition, Communication Skills, Rhetoric, The Uses of Language, The Art of Reading and Writing, and myriad others. Yet it has been inescapable; for a salutary re-study of the 1949 volume in its post-war context shows the pertinence of that context and reveals immediately how far "the field" has come in the past decade. Questions of direction and rate of evolution seem inevitable as teachers of English continue to assume responsibility for instruction in the major medium of human learning.

One change reported in the 1949 volume is particularly clear. In 1949, communication as a term applied to the teaching of English was a scant five years old (although it had been used as early as 1919 by the U. S. Office of Education). Lennox Grey in the National Council of Teachers of English pamphlet, *What Communication Means Today* (1944), had drawn into focus previously unrelated strands of inquiry and research in psychology, anthropology, political science, literary and art criticism, linguistics, media analysis and philosophy. In 1948 Lyman Bryson's important collection of essays, *The Communication of Ideas,* made the pertinence of this research to contemporary society amply clear. Also, by 1948, approximately two hundred colleges and universities had adopted the term communication in the titling or description of their freshman course — using varied designs and centers of interest. In the same year, seeking a working base for oral and written composition, the National Council of Teachers of English and the Speech Association of America jointly sponsored an exploratory meeting in Chicago. From this meeting there grew the Conference on College Composition and Communication, independent adjunct of the NCTE, and the National Society for the Study of Communication, independent adjunct of the SAA — but each concerned with improving instruction in the freshman course, and as inspection of ten years of convention agenda reveals, with the function of the freshman course within the designs of General Education programs.

Earl McGrath's 1949 volume reflected all of this with descriptions of courses in three state universities and three endowed institutions. Courses were chosen to represent clearly different approaches to the teaching of "Communication" — a strong concern for language as human symbol system (Drake, Minnesota) a

marked emphasis on descriptive linguistics (Drake), case analyses
of newspaper and radio as media for news dissemination (Minnesota, Colgate), patterns of relationship in the teaching of oral
and written composition (Illinois, Florida, Purdue). These descriptive statements were interspersed with essays on the teaching
of writing by principle, the urgency of instruction in listening, and
therapy of speech correction. The whole was framed, as it were,
by Lennox Grey's opening chapter pointing to the centrality of the
symbolic process to further maturation of communication as an
area of inquiry, and by Francis Shoemaker's concluding essay on the
common aesthetic concerns of the communication arts as "applied
contemporary humanities," and the older established Humanities
courses and programs.

The present volume, readers will discover, has a somewhat
similar design — with exploratory essays in five areas of inquiry
followed by descriptive accounts of courses on eighteen campuses.
These twenty-three statements have their roots firmly in the cultural context of the past decade — symbolized briefly by:

> . . . the virtual explosion of knowledge in linguistic research, from Fries' analysis of samples of spoken and written English to Whorf's exciting, hotly debated, hypothesis of the relation of linguistic structure to the perception of reality in a given culture;
>
> . . . the mounting interest in other "language arts" of rhetoric and logic as part of the simultaneously active rhetoric-logic-grammar involved in every communicative act, (a unity sometimes lost sight of on campuses where instruction in rhetoric is assumed by departments of speech, instruction in logic goes forward in departments of philosophy and mathematics, and instruction in grammar remains isolated in departments of English);
>
> . . . the NCTE publication of Lewis Leary's *Contemporary Literary Scholarship* (1958), speaking forcefully for a new kind of scholar-teacher-critic in the literatures of print and the public arts;
>
> . . . increased concern for the nature of the symbolic process to be seen in Susanne Langer's *Feeling and Form*, the neuro-physiology of D. O. Hebb at McGill, the psychiatric studies of Lawrence Kubie at Columbia, and Jurgen Ruesch at Berkeley, and related studies in vocal analysis of Paul J. Moses at California Institute of Technology, the anthropological-linguistic explorations of

intercultural understandings by Edward T. Hall — all providing further documentation for Sapir's early observation of "man's tendency to transform all experience symbolically";

. . . concern for expression in language and other arts in the development of fully matured persons, (whether described as "human potentialities" by Gardner Murphy, "becoming" by Gordon Allport, or "self-actualization" by Maslow and others) — with special attention to "creativity" as innovative behavior in science, art, politics, or education;

. . . the continuing "revolution" in the instruments of communication which play central roles in our culture — from the explosive spread of television into every home, to the dramatic rise of new information storage and "tutoring" and calculation machines;

. . . the closely related work of Lyman Bryson in this country and the earlier work of Harold Innis in Canada, both pointing out that changes in forms and channels of communication are at once index and agent of corresponding cultural change.

Here, indeed, is the intellectual climate of near-saturation, which, in the face of space-age quest for quick resolutions, has led some scholars to advocate return to "tradition" and others to seek more comprehensive designs for survival.

Much of this scholarship and cultural change has been reported elsewhere.[2] In including these seminal items in this volume, we hope to provide broad context for the contributions, in Part I, of five scholar-teachers to new concerns for the relation of scholarly method to teaching method in literature, media study, rhetoric, logic and grammar — and also for the descriptive statements, in Part II, of courses on representative campuses.

In Part I authors have approached their areas in interestingly diverse ways. Lennox Grey, taking his theme from the recent *Basic Issues in the Teaching of English*, examines the troublesome question of how students learn to write, looking particularly at the role of imitative writing in the process. Marshall McLuhan, assumes Innis' hypotheses in *Empire and Communications*, and moves

[2]Shoemaker, Francis (Ed.) *Communication and the Communication Arts.* New York: Bureau of Publications, Teachers College, Columbia University, 1955.

on to deal with the "grammars" of the newer media of radio, TV, film. Father Fogarty examines the newer rhetorics of Richards and Burke from the perspective of modern communication theory, finds remarkable parallels in rhetoric and communication, and proposes increased teaching of philosophy of language as the content encompassing acquisition of skills and arts of communication. Monroe Beardsley explores emerging approaches to logic with their concerns for patterns for interpretation and explanation as well as for proof. Freeman Twaddell, in describing the verb grammar of English, assumes the growing commitment to all viable structural data, but goes on to demonstrate how a linguist works in an area already replete with conventional concepts and terminologies — indeed, exemplifying a new definition of "describe" and "description" as the ultimate in scientific behavior. These scholarly essays serve several purposes. They provide considerable perspective for new instructional staff being recruited from among degree candidates on many campuses, not only on range of content but on scholarly method in its relation to teaching method in the several fields. They provide also a kind of definition of the frontiers of the freshman course, useful as touchstones for staffs continuing with broad scale or incremental revisions of current programs.

Part II constitutes an exciting tour of eighteen campuses. Schools have not been selected to exemplify special approaches to composition and communication. At this stage such hand-picking scarcely seemed like "descriptive" behavior. We started, rather, with the classification originally used to determine representation on the Executive Committee of the Conference on College Composition and Communication — the state university, the state college, the privately endowed institution, the technical institute, the community college, the United States Service Academy — from coast to coast, north and south. In only one of these schools, the Air University at Maxwell Air Force Base, are there no freshman students. We have broken step here to point up a clear recognition on the part of an advanced communication staff that even in graduate school no one has gone beyond improvement in the arts of communication.

No single course described attempts to deal with the whole field as represented in contemporary trends or the scholarship of the five major areas of concern, yet the field is represented in the aggregate. Looked at together, the courses show certain marked tendencies that may indeed presage directions of development. There is marked concern for literature, for whole works to be examined as imaginative formulations of values by authors addressing their contemporaries (Michigan State, Miami University, Vassar). Students are being led in audience studies, and at the same time in studies of the aesthetics of design through which authors have achieved self-realization in speaking to their cultures. The content in two such courses (Vassar, Berkeley) is British and American literature; in others (Morehouse, Michigan) it is American literature and world literature, and the history of ideas (Boston University Junior College) and the history of American ideals (West Point). Whatever the conventional classification, the courses are addressed to today's communication needs and may almost constitute a redefinition of "world literature" as any significant writing which contributes to responsible participation in the simultaneity of contemporary world culture. Several schools are explicitly aware of the total field of communication arts, skills and media; one (Carnegie) chooses within this context to center attention on writing; others (St. Cloud, Diablo) attempt to work through all three. There is, as might be anticipated, a persistent concern for study *of* and *about* language (Rensselaer), with some indication of growing liaison with foreign languages (Hampton), and repeated concern for rhetoric and logic as the arts which "create human relations" (Carnegie, Air University) and as the arts through which communication is adapted to varied purposes and realms of discourse (West Point, General Motors Institute, Boston University Junior College). This last seems particularly significant in view of the simultaneous publication of additional volumes in this series on General Education — in Social Sciences, in Natural Sciences, in the Humanities.

There are also rather clearly observable pointers in course organization and instructional procedure. There are numerous campuses on which the course no longer carries the full burden of instruction in communication skills but functions as one of several alternate requirements (Berkeley, Wayne) or as one of a cluster of courses which contribute in depth to proficiency in communication (M.I.T., Vassar, Michigan State). This fact seems to suggest that there is decreasing thought of the freshman course as a tool or service course, and increasing awareness of its having a body of content in language and language arts, and in communication concepts and media analysis that incorporates its own philosophy and internal scholarly method.   It is assuming a new role in General Education.

There is pervasive concern with preparation of new staff to meet demands of increasing enrolments, with considerable experimentation with class size and frequency of meetings (Iowa).   Three aspects of method are repeatedly referred to: the use of the "case study" .as leading to independent inquiry (Miami, Carnegie, Vassar, Hampton), the recognition of "discussion" as teaching method in the English class, and the utilization of the campus as the communication laboratory for reality-testing of proficiency and maturation in skill and self assurance (St. Cloud, Hampton).

It is difficult to break off this enumerative comment on striking features of contemporary instruction in composition and communication.   The field is alive!   And probably the clearest indication of the vitality is the across-the-board recognition of the vastly increased flow of new knowledge in the field, with which students are already conversant, and the readiness of staffs to come to grips with the problem of strategic selection of content which is visibly and viably pertinent to contemporary living — and the development of teaching method appropriate to it.   Probably the concluding note that speaks for every English staff is explicitly phrased by the staff at the Air University, where "officers are given opportunity to think into the future . . . . to see the world . . . . as it will be in five years' time or a decade."

Teachers College   Louis Forsdale
Columbia University   Francis Shoemaker
November, 1960

Part I

contemporary scholarship in
aspects of composition
and communication

chapter 1

"...LEARNING TO WRITE AND THE READING OF IMAGINATIVE LITERATURE..."

A Study in Scholarly Method and Teaching Method

*Lennox Grey**

1

Each generation has its educational issues of highest priority, and its own special combination of accents in speaking of them — variously purposeful, troubled, patient, urgent, sober, ironic, urbane, aggressive, defensive, condescending, aspiring — according to context and circumstance.

During the next generation no issue in our educational scene is likely to be of greater importance than what we do with and how we speak, purposefully or otherwise, of the recently published *Basic Issues in the Teaching of English* (1959), in which some thirty representative members of the Modern Language Association, the National Council of Teachers of English, the College English Association, and the American Studies Association, in a series of four cumulative and sequential meetings in January, April, June and October 1958, and in subsequent consultation and correspondence, have formulated a list of thirty-five numbered issues, with a preface and conclusion posing the large issue of what can be done about them by individuals, departments, organizations and foundations.

The document itself is a remarkable example of literate candor, as the following statement of one of our perennial questions in the teaching of college composition and communication will quickly indicate:

*Head, Department of the Teaching of English and Foreign Languages, Teachers College, Columbia University.

14. *What is the relation between learning to write and the reading of imaginative literature?* Although good writers are usually discriminating and sensitive readers, not all good readers write well. Some courses, and even some college departments, separate composition and literature from each other. Does the ability to write well come largely from exercises which reflect the student's own practical needs? And does too great dependence upon literary models produce an affected or too imitative style in student writers? Conversely, how can a student ever acquire a sensitiveness to language without studying literary works which illustrate such sensitiveness? Does the common course which includes both literature and composition tend to neglect one in favor of the other? If so, is this because we know too little about the relationship between them?

Probably the greatest danger in this and the other issues is that the number of major questions and sub-questions about which we "know too little" will loom so large that many of us will simply throw up our hands defensively — like a good scholarly friend of mine who asks in one breath "What's happening in your shop?" and then in another quick breath says "No, don't tell me — it'll only upset me!" Unquestionably, getting answers to these 35 Basic Issues questions and sub-questions will take a generation at least, with every device which departments, organizations and foundations can bring to them. But meanwhile, without waiting for a "massive breakthrough," are there some key aspects which individuals can get reasonably firm answers to, to confirm or revise suppositions and intuitions?

This chapter[1] aims to provide one small illustration of what may be done individually on the question of imitative writing, with means and methods congenial to most teachers of college English — specifically literary history and close critical reading, extended

---

[1]In the 1949 edition of *Communication in General Education* the writer of the present chapter dealt with problems of symbolic awareness in "No Signs, No Symbols! Uses A-B-C's." In ten years the developing of "symbolic awareness" in our students has been notably stimulated by the New Criticism, by anthropological ideas about "symbols of culture," and by communication research about "images" and "status symbols." Even the problem of the neurological basis of symbol-making may be on the way to solution in such books as D. O. Hebb's *The Organization of Behavior* (1949). And so, while symbolic awareness remains a key consideration, this chapter turns to another question of higher priority.

to a problem in teaching. An answer to the part of the question about imitative writing or "dependence on literary models" will not answer Issue 14 as a whole, but it can send a pencil of light through the center of it, focused on the commonly invoked sanctions for it and assumptions about it.

The first step will be to examine a piece of prior scholarship on the subject, undeservedly forgotten — "Robert Louis Stevenson Darkening Counsel" by Frank Aydelotte of Indiana University in *The English Journal* for June 1912, — which considers how far the "sedulous ape" experience of a literary artist is applicable to the mine-run of young Americans. A second, in keeping with familiar "sequential and cumulative" practices of scholarship, will be to see if this can be extended to a companion question Aydelotte does not undertake to answer: the significance of Benjamin Franklin's familiar observations about imitative writing for more characteristically "practical" American purposes. A final step will be to return from such sharply focused inquiry to the larger context of the problem, to see what bearings the first two steps have given.

2

Frank Aydelotte's "Robert Louis Stevenson Darkening Counsel" of 1912 would be worth including in this chapter and book if only to provide a useful foil, counterpoint, and historic dimension for the other chapters. It is high on my first nomination list for an historical anthology of little classics on the college teaching of English which I hope will be forthcoming. In all essentials it is a literary study, sticking to biographical and textual evidence for its conclusions. But it disposes completely of an educational sanction once widely derived from Stevenson, and it introduces an inviting possibility of another.

Aydelotte begins by getting us to look searchingly at what Stevenson said:

> In one of the most charming of all his personal essays — on "A College Magazine" — Robert Louis Stevenson outlines what is ordinarily called, in the oil-tainted slang of the composition class, the "sedulous ape" theory of learning to write. Plainly and clearly and with just enough detail, he tells us how he did it.
> "Whenever I read a book or a passage that particularly pleased me, in which a thing was said or an effect

rendered with propriety, in which there was either some
conspicuous force or some happy distinction in the style,
I must sit down at once and set myself to ape that quality.
I was unsuccessful, and I knew it; and tried again,
and was again unsuccessful and always unsuccessful; but
at least in these vain bouts, I got some practice in rhythm,
in harmony, in construction and the co-ordination of
parts.   I have thus played the sedulous ape to Hazlitt,
to Lamb, to Wordsworth, to Sir Thomas Browne, to
Defoe, to Hawthorne, to Montaigne, to Baudelaire and
to Obermann.   I remember one of these monkey tricks,
which was called *The Vanity of Morals* . . . written . . .
no less than three times: first in the manner of Hazlitt,
second in the manner of Ruskin, who had cast on me a
passing spell, and third, in a laborious pasticcio of Sir
Thomas Browne. . . .   Even at the age of thirteen I had
tried to do justice to the inhabitants of the famous city
of Peebles in the style of the *Book of Snobs*. . . .   But
enough has been said to show by what arts of impersona-
tion, and in what purely ventriloquial efforts I first saw
my words on paper."

Aydelotte quotes about twice the amount given here.   But
this is probably enough to show Stevenson's satirical comment on
his own method, and sets the tone and accent of Aydelotte's en-
suing comment.

According to that clear and definite method we have,
in this country, built up a great study of English composition. Thousands of teachers, using thousands of volumes
of carefully selected Models of Style, directed by thousands
of textbooks on Composition and the Art of Writing
(compendiums of analyzed and codified imitation) are at
work, teaching the American youth how to write.   It is
not all based on Stevenson of course.   He is not the only
"sedulous ape" in literature who has confessed, but he is
the arch-example.   [Benjamin Franklin was the other
chief confessor, but Aydelotte does not mention him for
reasons to be examined when we look at Franklin's
sanction.]   No author is so frequently quoted to the
aspiring high-school student or the sulky Freshman. Now
and then the long-tried undergraduate rebels.   I have
heard of a big Sophomore composition class at Harvard
which finally came to the point where they would stamp
whenever Stevenson's name was mentioned, as at the
mention of the Ladies or of Yale.

And yet, though we make the undergraduates imitate even to stamping, somehow it does not work. . . . Can it be that Stevenson was wrong, or is it that we do not follow him properly? . . .

We allow Stevenson to darken counsel for us in this matter of learning to write because we misunderstand and misrepresent him. Misreading his story of his own experience, we have built up a system of teaching which does not work because it is based on principles eternally false. We have overlooked the facts and misapplied his theories in the pseudo-scientific manner characteristic of our present-day study of the arts, to our own confusion. The facts we overlook are these: that Stevenson was a man filled with that energy and enthusiasm in the pursuit of his calling which we term genius; that he was a wide and intelligent reader; that his mind teemed with ideas; and that learning to write with him meant learning to say clearly, and therefore honestly, what he had to say. Ignoring all these facts we try to apply his method without discrimination to our undergraduates and high-school students who, for the most part, are neither readers nor thinkers, who have little to say, who have little desire to learn to write and no excuse for writing, and who need first of all to have their interests stimulated and broadened, to be taught to think and to read, rather than to be burdened with countless and wearisome exercises in the expression of such poor ideas as they have or can borrow. We have taken the plan which served the purposes of this brilliant Scotsman and tried to apply it to the whole American people, whose purposes it will not serve, and we are surprised that failure is the result.

Many years after his "sedulous ape" period, when Stevenson had learned his trade and was growing famous, he said exactly the thing about this matter of learning to write that I have been trying to make clear. When he was once . . . in Auckland, New Zealand, a newspaper reporter asked him what training he would advise for the young man who wished to learn to write. Stevenson's answer is published in the tenth chapter of *Stevensoniana*. It was, in three words, read, read, read. . . . .

When we have acquired some such respect for the business of writing we shall follow a different method in attempting to teach it. We shall . . . understand that a man has no call to write unless he has something to say, cannot learn otherwise, and ought not. We shall spend more time teaching our students to think, ask them to

write less and that more thoughtfully. And when we
find a student with ideas we shall not lower our standard
of adequate expression, but rather raise it, and, attempting what is worth while and also possible, let us hope
we shall have more success.

Mis-reading Stevenson has lead [sic] us astray in the
matter of English Composition, but the pity is not so
much that we should get from him something that is false
as that we should fail to get something that is true. . . .
Here was a man who knew how to read . . . To miss all
this in Stevenson for the sake of petty word-mongering
is to miss a fine and gracious account of the meaning
of literature from a man who knew how to read.

So Aydelotte makes clear that in the first generation of the
history of college composition there was (in the word of *The Basic
Issues*) "too great dependence upon literary models," based on a
premise and sanction proved faulty by scholarly examination,
though the effect was not primarily an "affected or too imitative
style." Evidently a return to such emphasis on that premise would
be justified neither by history nor by a critical reading of what
Stevenson said. Aydelotte's comment on having "something to say"
was then, and is now, a stock phrase of college composition instructors; but his suggestion that students read more and write
less ran counter to the "laboratory" notion (was this what he
meant by "pseudo-scientific"?) under which "composition" had
replaced the older theoretical rhetoric. Two comments from the
same year will illustrate pro's and con's on the laboratory concept:
"English composition, previously known as rhetoric, became osten-
sibly a laboratory course, but without any material addition to the
personnel of its teaching force," observes E. M. Hopkins' opening
article in the first issue, "Can Good Composition, and Teaching Be
Done Under Present Conditions?" (January, 1912) In an editorial
in the same issue, "Shall 'Laboratory Work' In Composition Be
Given Up?" appears the question, "Why not give laboratory principles an adequate test. . .?"

Something of the sort is done every day in newspaper offices — and, by the way, what would happen in
a newspaper office if the one managing editor were sud-
enly saddled with from a hundred to a hundred and fifty
cub reporters to break in all at once?

This whole "laboratory" premise needs re-examination: but not here.

Obviously Aydolette's attack does not dispose of the question of having *some* literary imitation. The question of Franklin's more workaday ideas and sanctions remains an obstacle to quick conclusions. Aydelotte's possible reasons for avoiding it are interesting to speculate on, and perhaps important. As a scholar with a sense of artistic unity, was he sticking to what he was sure he knew —Stevenson — and its bearing on the one aspect to which it would apply? Or did he avoid complicating the story with Franklin because (1) he knew this would open the other half of the problem, would double the length of the study, and would divide its force, or because (2) he knew that Franklin's *Autobiography*, as the chief other "confession," had become conspicuously unpopular with students (see "High-school Students' Rankings of English Classics," Charles Maxwell McCoury of the University of Illinois, in *The English Journal*, May, 1912 reporting the "condemnation of the *Autobiography*" with 112 out of 221 students placing it last in a list of 41 classics, and with a final rank of 35th out of 41) and was on the way out anyway? If so, it must have been with some regret, even so, that he passed up the chance for a little ironic notation about Franklin's admiration for *The Spectator*, on a passage from *Stevensoniana* which Aydelotte quotes:

> If a young man wishes to learn to write English he should read everything . . . the seventeenth century . . . the eighteenth century . . . Shakespeare . . . Thomas Browne . . . Jeremy Taylor . . . Dryden's prose and Samuel Johnson — and I suppose Addison, though I never read him myself . . . .

3

Franklin's *Autobiography*, which once every American high-school-boy used to know, takes on a rather different kind of significance as a guide to writing when read in the light of Aydelotte's article on Stevenson, from what it probably had when read in 1912 as a guide to practical morality — into which had been dropped an incident about a precocious young printer's apprentice imitating the *Spectator*. Presumably most teachers of 1912 who stressed practical morality ignored the fact that the *Autobiography* was written for the guidance of Franklin's natural son, and presumably

also they (and others since) ignored the fact, in using it as a guide
to imitative writing, that the passage on imitation is part of a
larger context that puts much more stress on (1) wide *reading* (as
with Stevenson) and (2) a discovery (as with others since) about
two-way communication which extended Franklin's concern considerably beyond those matters of grammar, vocabulary, and style
which had been focused primarily upon the written page.

Read in this way, the relevant parts of the *Autobiography*
become a second nominee for an anthology of classics on the
relation of reading to writing — providing us with further perspective and another foil which carries in itself the quality of scholarship and art which Aydelotte brought to his, and therefore calling
for only an occasional pointer to assure that we are looking at the
same things in it.

> From a child I was fond of reading, and all the
> little money that came into my hands was ever laid out
> in books . . . *Pilgrim's Progress* . . . John Bunyan's
> works in separate little volumes . . . R. Burton's *Historical
> Collections* . . . small chapman's books, and cheap, forty
> or fifty in all. My father's little library consisted chiefly
> of books in polemic divinity, most of which I read and
> have since often regretted that at a time when I had such
> a thirst for knowledge, more proper books had not fallen
> in my way, since it was now resolved that I should not
> be a clergyman. *Plutarch's Lives* there was . . . a book
> of Defoe's, called an *Essay on Projects,* and another of
> Dr. Mather's, called *Essays to do Good* . . . .
> This bookish inclination at length determined my
> father to make me a printer, though he had already one
> son (James) of that profession. . . . In a little time I
> made great proficiency in the business and became a useful
> hand to my brother. I now had access to better books.
> An acquaintance with the apprentices of booksellers en-
> abled me sometimes to borrow a small one, which I was
> careful to return soon and clean. Often I sat up in my
> room reading the greatest part of the night. . . .
> And after some time an ingenious tradesman, Mr.
> Matthew Adams, who had a pretty collection of books,
> and who frequented our printinghouse, took notice of me,
> invited me to his library, and very kindly lent me such
> books as I chose to read. I now took a fancy to poetry,
> and made some little pieces; my brother, thinking it might
> turn to account, encouraged me, and put me on composing

two occasional ballads. One was called *The Lighthouse
Tragedy* . . . the other was a sailor's song, on the taking
of Teach (or Blackbeard), the pirate. They were
wretched stuff, in the Grub-street-ballad style . . . The
first sold wonderfully . . . This flattered my vanity; but
my father discouraged me by ridiculing my performances
and telling me verse-makers were generally beggars. So I
escaped being a poet, most probably a very bad one; but
as prose writing has been of great use to me in the course
of my life, and was a principal means of my advancement,
I shall tell you how, in such a situation, I acquired what
little ability I have in that way.

As sanction, Franklin's words can hardly suffer the charge
of artistic impracticality which Aydelotte levelled against following
Stevenson's "counsel"; but it too grew out of motivations far
stronger than most American schoolboys and schoolgirls feel, either
to read or to write.

Significantly, Franklin continues by talking as much about
oral communication as about writing. And Franklin's father,
seldom cited in this connection, assumes increased importance as a
teacher:

There was another bookish lad in the town, John
Collins by name, with whom I was intimately acquainted.
We sometimes disputed; and very fond we were of argument, and very desirous of confuting one another, which
disputatious turn, by the way, is apt to become a very
bad habit, making people often extremely disagreeable
in company . . . and thence, besides souring and spoiling
the conversation, is productive of disgusts and, perhaps,
enmities where you may have occasion for friendship. I
had caught it by reading my father's books of dispute
about religion. Persons of good sense, I have since observed, seldom fall into it, except lawyers, university men,
and men of all sorts that have been bred at Edinburgh.

A question was once, somehow or other, started
between Collins and me of the propriety of educating the
female sex in learning, and their abilities for study. He
was of the opinon that it was improper, and that they
were naturally unequal to it. I took the contrary side,
perhaps a little for dispute's sake. He was naturally more
eloquent, had a ready plenty of words, and sometimes, as
I thought, bore me down more by his fluency than by
the strength of his reasons. As we parted without settling

the point, and were not to see one another again for some time, I sat down to put my arguments in writing, which I copied fair and sent to him. He answered, and I replied. Three or four letters of a side had passed, when my father happened to find my papers and read them. Without entering into the discussion, he took occasion to talk to me about the manner of my writing; observed that, though I had the advantage of my antagonist in correct spelling and pointing (which I owed to the printing-house), I fell far short in elegance of expression, in method, and in perspicuity, of which he convinced me by several instances. I saw the justice of his remarks, and thence grew more attentive to the *manner* in writing, and determined to endeavor at improvement.

So we have on record some apparently effective well-motivated early instruction in composition in America, by a teacher, incidentally, whom Benjamin Franklin often resented. Now comes the familiar sanctioning passage about imitating the *Spectator*, showing Franklin's usual ingenuity:

About this time I met with an odd volume of the *Spectator*. It was the third . . . I bought it, read it over and over, and was much delighted with it. I thought the writing excellent, and wished, if possible, to imitate it . . . I took some of the papers, and, making short hints of the sentiment in each sentence, laid them by a few days, and then, without looking at the book, tried to complete the papers again by expressing each hinted sentiment at length, and as fully as it had been expressed before, in any suitable words that should come to hand. Then I compared my *Spectator* with the original, discovered some of my faults, and corrected them. But I found I wanted a stock of words, or a readiness in recollecting and using them, which I thought I should have acquired before that time if I had gone on making verses; since the continual occasion for words of the same import, but of different length to suit the measure, or of different sound for the rhyme, would have laid me under a constant necessity of searching for variety and also have tended to fix that variety in my mind and make me master of it. Therefore, I took some of the tales and turned them into verse; and, after a time, when I had pretty well forgotten the prose, turned them back again. I also sometimes jumbled my collections of hints into confusion, and after some weeks endeavored to reduce them into the best order, before I

began to form the full sentences and complete the paper.
This was to teach me method in the arrangement of
thoughts. By comparing my work afterwards with the
original, I discovered many faults and amended them;
but I sometimes had the pleasure of fancying that in certain particulars of small import I had been lucky enough
to improve the method or the language, and this encouraged me to think I might possibly in time come to be a
tolerable English writer, of which I was extremely ambitious. My time for these exercises and for reading was
at night, after work, or before it began in the morning, or
on Sundays, when I contrived to be in the printing-house
alone. . . .

We make a mistake, though, if we stop our professional reading of the *Autobiography* there, as apparently most teachers have
stopped it. Two paragraphs later Franklin expands his earlier
observation about oral communication processes, and offers, as an
extra professional dividend, a comment on a grammar text which
constitutes one of the most ironic observations on record about what
had happened to the once three-fold "communication arts" of the
ancients as the rising middle classes of the eighteenth century sought
short cuts to "correctness" in speech as they sought "correctness"
in manners generally.

While I was intent on improving my language, I met
with an English grammar (I think it was Greenwood's),
at the end of which there were two little sketches of the
arts of rhetoric and logic, the latter finishing with a specimen of a dispute in the Socratic method; and soon after
I procured Xenophon's *Memorable Things of Socrates,*
wherein there are many instances of the same method.
I was charmed with it, adopted it, dropped my abrupt
contradiction and positive argumentation, and put on the
humble inquirer and doubter. And being then, from reading Shaftesbury and Collins, become a real doubter in
many points of our religious doctrine, I found this method
safest for myself and very embarrassing to those against
whom I used it; therefore I took a delight in it, practiced
it continually, and grew very artful and expert in drawing
people, even of superior knowledge, into concessions, the
consequences of which they did not foresee, entangling
them in difficulties out of which they could not extricate
themselves, and so obtaining victories that neither myself
nor my cause always deserved.

Happily, Franklin, having learned the power in knowing
something of the arts of communication, which had been relegated
to the back of the book, as distinct from the rules of grammar
which had been given the front of it (and which Franklin saw no
cause to mention further in saying how he learned to write and
communicate), also saw the dangers in their manipulations, as
today we see the dangers in dictators or advertisers manipulating
symbols.   Perhaps he would have seen them sooner if his father
had pointed them out to him as Benjamin Franklin was pointing
them out to his son.

> I continued this method some few years, but grad-
> ually left it, retaining only the habit of expressing myself
> in terms of modest diffidence. . . .   This habit, I believe,
> has been of great advantage to me when I have had occa-
> sion to inculcate my opinions and persuade men into meas-
> ures that I have been from time to time engaged in
> promoting; and, as the chief ends of conversation are to
> *inform* or to be *informed,* to *please* or to *persuade,* I wish
> well-meaning, sensible men would not lessen their power
> of doing good by a positive, assuming manner that seldom
> fails to disgust, tends to create opposition and to defeat
> every one of those purposes for which speech was given
> to us, to wit, giving or receiving information or pleasure.
> For if you would *inform,* a positive dogmatical manner in
> advancing your sentiments may provoke contradiction and
> prevent a candid attention.   If you wish information and
> improvement from the knowledge of others, and yet at the
> same time express yourself as firmly fixed in your present
> opinions, modest, sensible men, who do not love disputa-
> tion, will probably leave you undisturbed in the posses-
> sion of your error.

Wide reading — correspondence with a bookish friend —
a father's critical comments — ambition — a conception of two-
way communication — a little enthusiastic imitation; these, in this
order, seem to have been the chief ingredients in Franklin's learning to write.   And above all, as with Stevenson, wide reading —
and ambition.

4

From both Stevenson and Franklin, then, if their sanctions
are significant, it would seem that we should look particularly into

the possibilities of "read, read, read" and "write less, and that more thoughtfully." That does not mean write *little;* it means less blind "write, write . . ." If some such procedure should prove even *as good as* the long standing "laboratory composition" it might go a long way toward removing those conditions in Issue 32 which are directly opposed to the young scholar-teacher's taking time to work on the professional problem of "learning to write and the reading of imaginative literature":

> 32. *Can the teaching of composition be raised to the same level of academic respectability as the teaching of literature?* The teaching of composition is regarded as drudgery, is paid badly, and offers little opportunity for advancement in rank. Typically it is thought to be only a steppingstone to the teaching of literature. Teachers who share this attitude are not likely to inspire a love of English in their students. The morale of the freshman course is one of the most complex and important issues which confronts the profession.

Add to this the condescension toward much "methods" work, made the scapegoat for every kind of educational deficiency, and you have about as much anti-incentive as you could invent for keeping young scholars from it.

Yet in spite of these obstacles some scholars in every generation have felt that not to deal with these problems is itself unscholarly. And though we find very little that is cumulative and sequential in this scholarship — as our illustrative question in *The Basic Issues* testifies — there has been a very remarkable accumulation of "scholarship passing through," in no sense inferior to Aydelotte's. There is more than we realize in *The English Journal* 1912-1927, the "College Edition" 1928-1939, *College English* since 1939-40, *The Teaching of College English* (*1934*) edited for the NCTE by O. J. Campbell, the *Bulletin of the Conference on College Composition and Communication* since 1950, the *CEA Critic* since 1939, the college part of *The English Language Arts* (1952), and now *The Basic Issues in the Teaching of English* (1959).

At present, less than six months after nearly simultaneous issue by *PMLA*, *College English*, the *CEA Critic*, and *The American Quarterly*, the slender 16-page *Basic Issues* probably looms not much larger on the educational horizon than that symbolic "small cloud" in Virginia Woolf's *Orlando* foretelling the Victorian Era. To some it may have much the same symbolic portent, a "coming of the damp," — but now they will fear, threatening, not overdraped and overstuffed furnishings, but overdraped and overstuffed writing on professional "methods." (It can do just that, if left to "George," as W. R. Parker said in his 1959 MLA presidential address.) But to others it can be a sliver of light no wider than one's finger on a long clouded horizon, no less capable of growing and of bringing a scholarly illumination to problems of teaching than it has brought to literature and language. Such a shift of metaphor from the one most appropriate to Virginia Woolf's North Atlantic-North Sea-British Isles scene offers some problems, of course, but none that a mobile people used to going forth to seek the sun in a continental scene cannot make appropriate too. It can if the most able scholars take the trouble to show the way — on writing, reading, and all the rest, according to the skill of each.

chapter 2

GRAMMARS FOR THE NEWER MEDIA

*Marshall McLuhan**

When I began to teach Freshman rhetoric in 1936 the "new criticism" had not yet begun to be current in colleges. Nor had there yet begun that full study of ancient rhetoric as a means of understanding Renaissance literature. Moreover, the application of anthropological method to the appreciation of the multi-levelled riches of popular culture had not yet come into vogue. From the first, I used all three of these approaches to freshman English, and further, found the Basic English of Ogden and Richards a wonderful aid. To these I would add to-day an introduction to the "languages" of the various media of writing, typing, print, photography, film, radio, and television. For these tongues of the media, whether touched with mechanism or electronic fire, serve to reshape the patterns of discourse, and constitute a large portion of our "meaning."

What is shared by the "new criticism," by traditional rhetoric, popular culture, and by study of the languages and grammars of the media, is the habit of reading and writing *in depth*. Depth analysis ended with printing and has returned in the past century, which may become known as the electric or electronic age. Multi-levelled exegesis of Ovid or Virgil or the Scriptures was not only a medieval mode of reading and writing. It preceded Christianity and was the norm among ancient "grammarians." To-day it is again the norm in physics, in psychology, in poetry and the arts.

---

*Professor of English, St. Michael's College, University of Toronto.

Why then should the art of printing have interrupted this procedure for three or four centuries?

The power of print to impose its own assumptions on many areas of action and experience is the answer to the last question. And just what were the assumptions of print, was as obscure to the first ages of printing as the assumptions of television are to us all at present. For the assumptions of any new structure are seldom if ever verbal. They are revealed usually by conflict with earlier or later structures. Thus, printing which appeared at first as a cheaper and more easily read kind of manuscript came into direct clash with the oral schoolmen, and with Church and political authorities. Print offered a new kind of knowledge of the world and of self and society. It moved information very fast, in segments that followed in even lines on single planes. Print technology proceeded by mechanizing the old handicraft of the scribe. This it did by breaking up the art of writing into separate movable types which could make uniform and endlessly repeatable images of letters. In short, by taking one thing at a time, print technology showed us how to get command of many other areas of action and experience. There is a celebrated passage in Ben Franklin's *Autobiography* which illustrates how print had inspired new methods even in the interior spirituality and morality of the seventeenth and eighteenth century men:

"It was about this time I conceived the bold and arduous project of arriving at moral perfection. I wished to live without committing any fault at any time; I would conquer all that either natural inclination, custom, or company might lead me into. As I knew, or thought I knew, what was right and wrong, I did not see why I might not always do the one and avoid the other. But I soon found I had undertaken a task of more difficulty than I had imagined. While my care was employed in guarding against one fault, I was often surprised by another; habit took the advantage of inattentioin; inclination was sometimes too strong for reason. I concluded, at length, that the mere speculative conviction that it was our interest to be completely virtuous was not sufficient to prevent our slipping; and that the contrary habits must be broken, and good ones acquired and established, before we can have any dependence on a steady, uniform rectitude of conduct. For this purpose I therefore contrived the following method. . . ."

. . . . "My intention being to acquire the *habitude* of all these virtues, I judged it would be well not to distract my attention by attempting the whole at once, but to fix it on one of them at a time; and, when I should be master of that, then to proceed to another, and so on, till I should have gone through the thirteen; and, as the previous acquisition of some might facilitate the acquisition of certain others, I arranged them with that view, as they stand above. *Temperance* first, as it tends to procure that coolness and clearness of head, which is so necessary where constant vigilance was to be kept up, and guard maintained against the unremitting attraction of ancient habits, and the force of perpetual temptations. This being acquired and established, *Silence* would be more easy, and my desire being to gain knowledge at the same time that I improved in virtue, and considering that in conversation it was obtained rather by the use of the ears than of the tongue, and therefore wishing to break a habit I was getting into of prattling, punning, and joking, which only made me acceptable to trifling company, I gave *Silence* the second place. This and the next *Order*, I expected would allow me more time for attending to my project and my studies. *Resolution*, once become habitual, would keep me firm in my endeavors to obtain all the subsequent virtues; *Frugality* and *Industry* freeing me from my remaining debt, and producing affluence and independence, would make more easy the practice of *Sincerity* and *Justice*, etc., etc. Conceiving then, that, agreeably to the advice of Pythagoras in his Golden Verses, daily examination would be necessary, I contrived the following method for conducting the examination."

"I made a little book, in which I allotted a page for each of the virtues. I ruled each page with red ink, so as to have seven columns, one for each day of the week, marking each column with a letter for the day. I crossed these columns with thirteen red lines, marking the beginning of each line with the first letter of one of the virtues, on which line, and in its proper column, I might mark, by a little black spot, every fault I found upon examination to have been committed respecting that virtue upon that day."

"I determined to give a week's strict attention to each of the virtues successively. Thus, in the first week, my great guard was to avoid every the least offense against *Temperance*, leaving the other virtues to their ordinary chance, only marking every evening

the faults of the day. Thus, if in the first week I could keep my
first line, marked T, clear of spots, I supposed the habit of that
virtue so much strengthened, and its opposite weakened, that I
might venture extending my attention to include the next, and for
the following week keep both lines clear of spots. Proceeding
thus to the last, I could go through a course complete in thirteen
weeks, and four courses in a year. And like him who, having
a garden to weed, does not attempt to eradicate all the bad herbs
at once, which would exceed his reach and his strength, but works
on one of the beds at a time, and, having accomplished the first,
proceeds to the second, so I should have, I hoped, the encouraging
pleasure of seeing on my pages the progress I made in virtue, by
clearing successively my lines of their spots, till in the end, by a
number of courses, I should be happy in viewing a clean book,
after a thirteen weeks' daily examination."

A passage from William Cobbett's *A Year's Residence in America* (1795) reveals the effect of print culture on the personal and
emotional lives of men at the same period. Cobbett is describing
the new American in contrast to the Englishman who has not yet
gone all out for literacy:

"There are very few really *ignorant* men in America of native
growth. Every farmer is more or less of a *reader*. There is no
brogue, no provincial dialect. No class like that which the French
call *peasantry* . . . . they are all well-informed; modest without
shyness; always free to communicate what they know, and never
ashamed to acknowledge they have yet to learn. You never hear
them *boast* of their possessions, and you never hear them *complain-
ing* of their wants. They have all been readers from their youth
up; and there are few subjects on which they cannot converse with
you whether of a political or a scientific nature. At any rate they
always *hear* with patience. I do not know that I ever heard a native
American interrupt another man while he was speaking. Their
sedateness and *coolness*, the *deliberate* manner in which they say
and do everything, and the *slowness* and *reserve* with which they
express their assent; these are very wrongly estimated when they are
taken for marks of a *want* of *feeling*. It must be a tale of woe
indeed, that will bring a tear from an American's eye; but any
trumped-up story will send his hand to his pocket . . . However, you
will not, for a long while, know what to do for want of the
quick responses of the English tongue, and the decided tone of the

English expression.   The *loud voice* and the *hard squeeze* by the hand; the *instant assent* or *dissent;* the clamorous joy, the bitter *wailing;* the ardent friendship, the deadly enmity, the love that makes people kill themselves; the hatred that makes them kill others. All these belong to the characters of Englishmen, in whose minds and hearts every feeling exists in the *extreme."*

The same lineal procedures applied to the utilization of natural resources and the organization of citizen armies, enabled men to extend the methods of the assembly-line to every phase of national power and social order.

To-day the advent of exactly synchronized electronic tapes in industry has ended the regime of the assembly-line.   The same tapes have permitted the organization of structural linguistics which calls in question all the visual organization of speech and discourse which we have long known as "grammar."

The world of electronic information movement is an all-at-once world.   That is why in accepting it at all we abandon some of the assumptions of printing which include one-thing-at-a-timeness and indicate that words shall have one meaning at a time, and that discourse shall move on one plane at a time.   Even a century after printing, authors like Nashe and Montaigne retained the right to shift tone to reader and attitude to subject in mid-sentence and as often as they chose.   We now take for granted that writers shall maintain a consistent "point of view" and a single tone to reader and a single attitude to their subject.   But this procedure was unknown before the level, even flow of print which even so, writers were slow to exploit.   Perhaps it was not until Addison and Steele that an even tenor was hit upon as a mode of prose.   In Defoe and Swift this even tenor was used dead-pan for satirical effect.   With Blake and Burke and the Romantics the reaction against the levelling effects of print on the modes of human association and of thought came with intensity but with no effect upon the course of events. A celebrated passage in Burke's *French Revolution* serves to focus both the old world of status based on oral loyalty and the new world of contract based on the printed word:

"It is now sixteen or seventeen years since I saw the queen of France, then the dauphiness, at Versailles; and surely never lighted on this orb, which she hardly seemed to touch, a more delightful vision.   I saw her just above the horizon, decorating and cheering the elevated sphere she just began to move in, —

glittering like the morning-star, full of life, and splendour and joy.
Oh! what a revolution! and what a heart must I have to contem-
plate without emotion that elevation and that fall! Little did I
dream when she added titles of veneration to those of enthusiastic,
distant, respectful love, that she should ever be obliged to carry
the sharp antidote against disgrace concealed in that bosom; little
did I dream that I should have lived to see such disasters fallen
upon her in a nation of gallant men, in a nation of men of honour,
and of cavaliers. I thought ten thousand swords must have leaped
from their scabbards to avenge even a look that threatened her with
insult. But the age of chivalry is gone. That of sophisters, economists, and calculators, has succeeded; and the glory of Europe is
extinguished for ever. Never, never more shall we behold that
generous loyalty to rank and sex, that proud submission, that dig-
nified obedience, that subordination of the heart, which kept alive,
even in servitude itself, the spirit of an exalted freedom. The un-
brought grace of life, the cheap defence of nations, the nurse of man-
ly sentiment and heroic enterprise, is gone! It is gone, that sensibility
of principle, that charity of honor, which felt a stain like a wound,
which inspired courage whilst it mitigated ferocity, which ennobled
whatever it touched, and under which vice itself lost half its evil,
by losing all its grossness.''

To-day it is necessary to grasp the patterns of influence
exerted by the forms of print upon the habits of human perception
and feeling and action. Because, the printed word no longer exerts
its old force when it must share human attention with photo, film,
telephone, radio and television. Many new habits of perception
and attention which remain unverbalized, are now co-existent with
the older habits of perception of the earlier phases of print culture.
The teacher of literature to-day must be quite at home, must acquire literacy in these new modes of perception if the printed word
in prose or poetry is to be taught effectively. Nor is it very difficult
to acquire ease in these new modes of experience. For our poets
began a century ago to prepare us for the change from the monarchy
of print to the oligarchy of print and press and photo and film
and radio and television. Artists in general and in all ages are
engaged in grappling directly with the ever new problems of experience resulting from technological change. Scott and Byron
explored the photographic and movie possibilities of language and
narrative long before photography and film. Crabbe, Dickens and

Browning adapted the new medium of the press to artistic ends of human interest and group reporting before newspapers had got onto the same track.   Edgar Poe was the first artist of the electronic age as it were.   In both prose and verse he invented the do-it-yourself forms which now are taken for granted as the necessary forms of a world electrically wired.   That is to say that his symbolist technique in poetry brings the reader directly into the poetic process.   The reader of symbolist poetry like the viewer of cubist painting must in large degree make the work himself.   The poem or painting becomes not a consumer package but a do-it-yourself kit.   In prose, the detective story invented by Poe likewise invites the reader to be co-author page by page.   Hopkins and Baudelaire anticipated the modalities of the television world in language just as Seurat and Rouault did in painting.   (As Wyndham Lewis put it, "The artist is engaged in writing a detailed history of the future because he is aware of the unused possibilities of the present.") Most people are blocked in their intake of present experience by the back-log of assumptions derived from earlier experience.   Thus, the artist serves literally as *seer*, as one who can see exactly what is in front of him.

Hopkins came up with the notion and practice of *inscape* by way of contrast with landscape.   For a century the poets had been rendering experience via landscape, varying the inner emotions and feelings by this external means.   Hopkins was the first English poet to shift to inner landscape, "le paysage intérieure," which is not so much light *on* a scene as light *through* a scene.   The illumination is from within.   Joyce was later to dub this mode of awareness "epiphanies."

Rimbaud built his *Illuminations* on the same principle.   Baudelaire shifted the same principle to direct verbal meaning in his address to the reader of *Fleurs due Mal* as "Hypocrite lecteur, mon semblable mon frère!"

Instead of regarding the reader as one to whom the poet's voice is directed, Baudelaire announced that the poet as voice of the tribe heard and uttered his own words *through* the reader. T. S. Eliot proceeded to extend this principle in *The Waste Land* by means of Tiresias and with his concept of the poet not as one who expresses *himself* but as a catalyst.

The same principle of light through rather than light on, which is the difference between television image and movie or photographic image, appears in the painting of Seurat and Rouault long before television. Rouault's use of stained glass, like the Victorian Kaleidoscope, insists upon this new orientation of experience in which there is neither point-of-view nor three dimensions. But the two-dimensional can suggest many and three dimensional effects are only three dimensional.

We need to consider that the artists are not recording a private world of their own, but rather that they are articulating the world in which we are all living but in which very few of us can think or feel. The artist really thinks and feels in terms of the actual situation. He is a specialist in using his senses and in making pilot-models which enable the rest of us to catch up with our everyday world. The artist is not an ivory tower but a control tower personage, as even modern commerce has begun to understand. For several decades the artist has denied to. the audience the mere consumer privilege of passive day-dreaming experience. He has urged the audience to participate in the creative process with all its arduous excitement.

For many people this is very confusing. But so is ordinary living. The child who from one to six years experiences an adult world in front of television is sent to school at six. He experiences there a carefully prepared child world for the first time in his life. This is very confusing. Most children may never recover from this traumatic experience which began only ten years ago. We refer to it as "loss of motivation." As long as printing and industrial processes were parallel, a person could keep his bearings in the Western world. To-day our educational establishment has not come into rapport with our own technology, and there is little civil defense against media fall-out.

The college program in freshman English, that is to say, cannot realistically continue to teach just one grammar or rhetoric. When print was the norm of experience a single grammar could be taught. To-day even in the matter of the printed word critics and scholars insist on a multi-levelled approach to language. They point out that language is a far more complex structure than any known to physics or mathematics. Since all students already possess this structure, school and college must begin with a systematic description of what it is. The student can be shown how he speaks, what noises and verbal gestures he typically makes. By mere into-

nation we early give commands, ask questions, and make statements. Normative grammar and rhetoric based on the patterns of
print would naturally follow rather than precede an introduction
to our new linguistics. And linguistics was made possible by electronic tapes.

However, the role of structural linguistics in acquainting the
student with the richness of the speech he already has mastered is
naturally extendable into awareness of the dynamic language structures he has also picked up from various media besides his mother
tongue. By far the largest obstacles to student training to-day are
those resulting from subliminal backlog of media experience —
including print. Carl Orff, the Viennese composer, will not permit
any child who has learned to read or write to enter his school of
music. He claims that full musical training is forever frustrated
in a person who has been given a prior bias of the eye by the printed
word. Whether mistaken or not Orff is a beacon of orientation for
anybody attempting to teach language to-day at any stage or level
of instruction. Perhaps print is even more of an obstacle for those
entering mathematics and physics than for those in music. Vis-
ualization is a habit that must be unlearned in mathematics and
physics to-day. And this knowledge in turn helps us in literary
training to note and to stress the especial properties of our medium.
To-day we must not only know how to teach the inter-relationship
of speech, prose writing, and poetry. We must know how all
these are affected by the telephone and the typewriter, not to
mention the larger media. As T. S. Eliot has said: "When the
written language remains fixed, while the spoken language, the
vulgar speech, is undergoing change, it must ultimately be replaced
by a new written language, founded on current speech. Now the
language of prose is ordinarily nearer to that of speech than is the
language of poetry; so that if poetry arrogates the right to idiom,
vocabulary and syntax different from that of prose, it may eventually become so artificial as no longer to be able to convey living
feeling and living thought."

I think that the problem stated here by Eliot is enormously
complicated by television as a form of experience. And it no longer
needs to be urged that radio, movie, and television are not audio-
visual *aids* but special languages, with their own messages quite
regardless of program "content." The monarchy of print although

archaic, has left us with the idea that education can be conducted
on one plane at a time and in terms of one language or medium
at a time. This may be an ideal state for educators. It did actually
exist in the eighteenth and nineteenth centuries. But it is not
extant to-day.

Consider the plight of the business executive to-day who is
sent back to school at forty-five years of age. The traumatic shock
is almost as great for him as for the child taken out of his adult
television world and put into grade school. Why does big business
have to send its successful executives back to school? The answer
in a word is the telephone. This is a matter which nearly concerns the teacher of English. Because, until the telephone the rigid
structure of delegated authority in business remained intact. Delegated authority was a hierarchy of decision-making powers based
on written instructions and inter-office memos. The telephone
cut right across all this hierarchy. Nobody can exercise mere delegated authority by telephone. He can only exercise the "authority
of knowledge." Therefore he has to know the over-all operations
of his firm. Further, he has to understand the relation of his firm
to the over-all social and political fields. Therefore he has to go
back to school and try to acquire a liberal education. There is no
idealism in the blossoming of management centers to-day. They
are from necessity.

Now if such a small factor as the telephone can shake all the
corporation empires from top to bottom, we can, indirectly, form
some notion of how total a revolution faces our educational procedures and curricula from the impact of the larger and newer media.
Yet, just because language is the most complex of all man-made structures, it also embodies the largest amount of human skill
and experience. From any point of view then, language training
is the key to skill in all other structures, provided that such training
is co-extensive with the many levels of language. An approach to
language to-day in terms of print and visual order and meaning
alone will quite naturally be rejected by students. For students
to-day approach their world via languages of several media. That
is to say, that they live in a world that requires of them extremely
complex responses. Another way of saying this is to point to the
fact that in an electronic world there can be no hidden crannies or
any unarticulated experience. We cannot live with the subliminal
or the inarticulate in private or group experience.

We must be prepared to explore language not just in terms of an archaic print culture but in terms of language itself. Freshman English is still a frontier world.

chapter 3

A NEW LOOK AT RHETORIC

*Daniel Fogarty, S.J.**

There was a time when rhetoric was in formal dress. It was very strictly concerned with speech-making of the white tie and tails variety. If rhetoric was your line, then you were either a platform or pulpit orator, or you were involved in educating such orators. But for a long time now, rhetoric has worn informal attire. It appears in anything at all from swim-trunks to a grey flannel suit. Today we attempt to educate people for the whole range of their communicative activity. They need an art of expression that prepares them for plain, everyday talk as well as for a service club luncheon speech. And rhetoric (or composition, communication or English I) is lately beginning to try to provide this art. The point, of course, is that rhetoric is wherever people are: in the back yard in a plaid shirt, in the kitchen wearing a robe, or wearing a pinafore at a school picnic. Its subject, its topic, can be anything at all from apologizing or saying "Thank you" from a fire-escape window to proposing marriage across a restaurant table. The up-shot of all this is that rhetoric has very nearly become the art of universal communication.

Like all revolutionary ideas, this new view of rhetoric has driven its students back to an examination of the presuppositions underlying it, back to what might be called a philosophy of rhetoric or of communication. Connecting philosophy and rhetoric, Maurice Natanson says:

---

*Dean, School of Education, Saint Mary's University, Halifax, Nova Scotia.

> The need for re-examination of the nature and scope of rhetoric is voiced in many and diverse quarters today. . . .[1]

Students of rhetoric have gone deeper than oratory or the ancient practice of rhetoric, even beneath composition or the teaching of rhetoric, to the psychological and epistemological presuppositions that both the practice and the theory depend upon.   Here they seem to have found much that fulfills the present-day needs for a new rhetoric in the classroom.   This chapter proposes to review the most stimulating of these philosophical elements as seen by these same students of rhetoric.

Before the review of the new philosophical thinking about rhetoric, a glance at its history will be in order.[2]   It will serve both as a setting for the new rhetoric and as a confirmation of the avowed identity between rhetoric and the art of universal communication.

Rhetoric, in the earliest recorded accounts, was either a sophistic display of word manipulation or the art of pleading cases in court. Only with Plato and Aristotle did it become the ethical art of persuasion for oratorical purposes.   When the centre of culture moved from Athens to Rome, rhetoric moved with it and enjoyed Cicero's favor in the Senate as well as Quintilian's in the classroom.   In medieval times it was academically recognized as one of the seven liberal arts.   The Renaissance and specifically Bacon's influence broadened its scope far beyond its classical role as stylized oratory until it became the prose medium for the various types of the communication of ideas and information.   As such, rhetoric fulfilled itself until the turn of the nineteenth century when, at least in America, emphasis upon correctness of expression had begun to obliterate the once clear division between rhetoric and grammar.   It was at this point, when the practice and teaching of rhetoric lay dying, that its spirit, its philosophy, began to rise in many new forms. Interest in the problems of meaning, motivation and word symbolism, sparked by the new social sciences, began to produce the

---

[1]Natanson, Maurice, "The Limits of Rhetoric," *The Quarterly Journal of Speech*, XLI, (April, 1955), p. 135.

[2]Fogarty, Daniel, *Roots for A New Rhetoric* (New York: Teachers College Bureau of Publications, Columbia University, 1959), *Passim*. (Editors' note: Much of Father Fogarty's chapter here stems from his recent book.)

kind of thoughtfulness about the philosophical roots of communication that might be called a revival of rhetoric.[3]

Among the several current thinkers who provide such thoughtful insights two have seemed particularly rewarding: Professor I. A.
Richards of the Linguistic Institute at Harvard, poet, literary critic
and linguist, and Kenneth Burke of Bennington College, literary
critic, wandering lecturer and experimental novelist. Other contributors to the thoughtfulness of the new rhetoric have been
grouped together under one section.

I. A. RICHARDS

For such a brief synopsis as this, perhaps the most salient
features of Richards' philosophy of rhetoric would be: word-
thought-thing relationships; abstractions; and the theory of comprehending.

Underlying Richards' theory of relations between thoughts,
words and things is his notion of psychological context. In *The
Meaning of Meaning,* which he co-authored with C. K. Ogden, he
describes it as the whole complex network of mental, emotional,
sense and neural events that the subject may have connected with the
thing in question.[4] A match-scrape, for instance, has for psychological context, all the thought-content, feelings and neural responses ever connected by the subject with striking a match. The
odor of sulphur, the sound of the scrape, the sudden, small burst
of light together with the myriad associations that the subject might
have whimsically made with this event each and any time it happened to him. This can, of course, include frosty air or warm,
fireside sights and sounds and so on. All this complexity of
psychological context must enrich the thought itself of the match-
scrape. It makes my thought of a match-scrape vastly different
from anyone else's.

This, in Richards' thinking, explains the variability and ever
expanding breadth of the thought that goes with the thing and
its word.[5] For one word there are as many different thoughts as
there are persons to think them. The communicator must face as

---

[3]Burke, Kenneth, "Rhetoric Old and New," *The Journal of General Education,* V, (April, 1951), p. 203.

[4]Ogden, C. K., and I. A. Richards, *The Meaning of Meaning* (London:
Routledge and Kegan Paul Ltd., 1923), p. 52.

[5]*Ibid.,* p. 12.

many interpretations of his words as he has hearers or readers and even each of these is momentarily changing.   The word "alcohol" can immediately mean: "the curse of the family," "relaxed environment for conversation," "celebration," or "forgetfulness."   It depends on who is thinking about it whether it functionally comes closer to pre-dinner affability than to a night ward in Bellevue Hospital.   This, of course, leaves room for unethical uses of meaning in political and confidence-man rhetoric.   It can explain ambiguities, word-shifting, arguments that never get settled because the participants are at odds over names rather than things.   As Richards says, this is all due to faulty relationships between words and things:

> We shall find, however, that the kind of simplification typified by this once universal theory of direct meaning relations between words and things is the source of almost all the difficulties which thought encounters.[6]

Fundamental clarity of expression for the freshman student in our classrooms would seem to require some appreciation of this meaning problem.

The second facet of Richards' studies also leans heavily on his notion of psychological context but adds a new element.   His idea of abstraction is, by and large, the same as it has been understood since Aristotle.   But he begins differently.   He starts off with William James' notion of "primordial abstraction."[7]   Even the simplest forms of life are perpetually making what amount to selections, though they have no nervous systems nor any sensation or thinking power.   They move away from colder water to warmer, react defensively to invasion, shrink or expand to adjust to environment.   And in each movement they are saying, in their own primordial way: "Yes" or "No" to one or other situation.   For higher forms of life like man, this means selecting mentally or classifying.   And classifying is, of course, the process that makes possible the natural human talent for abstraction.[8]   Since abstraction is nothing much more than the selection of a quality from a real thing and applying it to a whole class of real things, and since

---

[6]Ogden and Richards, *op. cit.*, p. 12.

[7]Richards, I. A., *The Philosophy of Rhetoric* (New York: Oxford University Press, c1936), pp. 30-37.

[8]*Ibid.*, pp. 92-93.

primordial abstraction is somewhat the same thing for simpler forms
of life, Richards reasons that some of our human abstractions and
classifications have a lot to do with our more elemental and primordial urges.[9]   He might say that we think and classify and
abstract not only with our heads, but often with our hearts and
our feelings and our biological drives.

It is because our needs and feelings get so mixed up with our
rational thinking that we often cannot tell where our verbal deliberations have come from.   And it is this that makes necessary
what Richards calls the ἀρχή or governing reason:

> Richards' answer to the complexity of choice in the ab-
> stractive process is the ἀρχή, reason, whose function it
> is to control both the emotional and the conceptual ele-
> ments in the process in a way that insures the proper,
> realistic and balanced, whole meaning of the event.   It
> is under the guidance and control of reason that the pro-
> cess of abstraction can produce true and realistic abstract
> symbols.[10]

We must sift with our reason the animality and emotionality from
the rationality of our thinking and talking so as to watch over
it and see to it that our deliberations and actions are conformable
to truth.

These two facets of Richards' thinking lead him, along with
his other deliberations, to a theory that approaches the problem of
comprehending.   His interest is in the reception phase of communication.   He wants to know what are the underlying factors in
communicability.   He feels he has explored the reasons for ambiguity and word-shifting, variability of meaning and emotional
connotation.   Now he applies the results of these explorations to
the well known theory of communication as found, for instance,
in the Shannon-Weaver formula.[11]   This provides, for Richards,
a set of normative implements for interpreting communication, what
he calls his seven instruments of comprehending.[12].   The seven
instruments were evolved from the seven elements of meaning in any
unit of communication: Indicating, Characterizing, Realizing, Val-

---

[9]*Ibid., pp.* 30-34.

[10]Fogarty, *op. cit.,* p. 35.

[11]Richards. I. A., *Speculative Instruments* (Chicago: The University of
Chicago Press, 1955), pp. 23-37.

[12]*Ibid.,* p. 26.

uing, Influencing, Controlling and Purposing. The mutual control of all seven is the ἀρχή or ruling element and all seven can
be translated into questions that the receiver of the communication may ask himself so as to gauge the efficiency of his own reception of the communicated unit.[13] Supplementation of this sketchy
outline of Richards' theory of comprehending may be found
throughout the second chapter of his *Speculative Instruments*. It
should be remembered too that Richards is a teacher and it was
precisely with undergraduate students that he tested and refined
his seven elements of meaning.[14]

KENNETH BURKE

Kenneth Burke, the second exponent of a philosophy for a
new rhetoric, approached it, like Richards, from the receiver's point
of view. But while Richards' point of departure was in some
respects bio-psychological, Burke's was socio-psychological.[15] He
was interested in the reception of meaning and saw that it was
often fragmentary and misconceived if not missed altogether. So
he began to analyze the social and psychological factors that might
make one person's meaning for a term differ from another's. There
is space here for only two of his many insights: one concerns his
general method of garnering all or most of the meaning of a communication and he calls it his "pentad format." The other deals
with motivation and the havoc this may play with the conventional
meaning of terms.

The pentad format is really a general philosophical formula
for studying anything as well as a manner of tackling the interpretation of a communication.[16] It sets up five aspects under which
may be listed all that can be known about anything at all. The
aspects are: *scene, act, agent, agency* and *purpose*.[17] There is but
a thin difference between this pentad and the four ultimate causes
used by Aristotle and the Scholastic Philosophers in their inquiries.
Even the scientific elements of communication called: Source, Chan-

---

[13]*Ibid.*, p. 27.

[14]Richards, I. A., *Practical Criticism* (New York: Harcourt, Brace and Co.,
c1929), Intro., pp. 1-6.

[15]Fogarty, *op. cit.*, pp. 56-59.

[16]Burke, Kenneth, *A Grammar of Motives* (New York: Prentice-Hall Inc.,
1945), Intro. p. xv.

[17]*Ibid.*, pp. xv-xxiii.

nel, Receiver and Purpose are not evidently different.   And the old-
time journalist's rule-of-thumb for covering a story, the "who,
when, where, how and why" seems much the same.   But the Bur-
keian pentad, when put to work on a communication unit, in its
question form, is bound to yield worlds more meaning than the
usual question "What does it mean?"   Can you imagine what
answers await the freshman in your classroom when he asks himself why Hamlet sent Ophelia away?   Information about the whole
context of Hamlet's life and surroundings answers the question:
"What was the scene of this act?"   Separate thought given to the
act itself, to the reasons in Hamlet's mind for doing it, to the way
he did it, to the feelings and motives he had and the interior conflicts that caused it, would be bound to illuminate the action as
never before.   Can you also imagine what understanding and cooperation might stem from a like procedure whenever there was
question of condemning someone's statements made in ordinary
conversation?

     The complexity of motivation for the simplest human acts
and the extent of the role it plays in communication have im-
pressed Burke a great deal.[18]   There are ennobling, excusing, ra-
tionalizing phrases in great abundance in ordinary communication.
They window-dress the individual and hide all the less acceptable
motives not only from others but, more important, from himself.
The example of the two bank clerks is illustrative.   One threw up
his job and eloped with an unacceptable lady.   His explanation
to himself said he did it "for love."   Another bank clerk in very
similar circumstances stayed at his job and beamed at the com-
pliments paid him for his reliability because he did what he did
"for duty's sake."   This sort of ambiguous and readily adjustable
naming not only calls for a careful study of motivated definition
in any kind of communication course but seems to underline the
inadequacy of the usual courses in composition.   Burke's books
abound in examples of these and other manifestations of words
meaning more than they seem to say. Some of the socio-
psychological attitudes we all seem to have make us describe things
with the slant that our feelings dictate rather than the objectivity
we think we are exercising.   The worker calls his assembly-line

---

     [18]Burke, Kenneth, *Permanence and Change* (Los Altos, California: Hermes
Publications, 1954) rev. ed. pp. 19-36 and 216-236.

job "regimentation." The industrialist who hires him may call it "planned economy."[19] With these and other insights Burke points to the necessity of seeing the many facets of one communication, the many viewpoints of partisan debate, so that the mind, seeing all the opinions can come to that kind of honorable compromise that springs from understanding and leads to peaceful and constructive action. With the application of the new insights into motivation and the use of the pentad format, a man can sit inside his own interior parliament and hear the whole series of different approaches, partisan speeches, and come to a wise conclusion well weighted with truth. As Burke himself says:

> Ideally, all the various "voices" are partisan rhetoricians whose partial voices "competitively cooperate" to form the position of the dialogue as a whole (a position that transcends all the partial views of the participants, though there may be a Socratic voice that is "primus inter pares.").[20]

This depth and wisdom can be gleaned by anyone for himself through a study of Burke's methods. And more, the application of such ideas to discussion techniques as taught in freshman courses is evidently weighted with possibilities.

Richards and Burke must be left here. But a more leisurely and first-hand perusal of their works will reward all who have caught, in these few lines, the challenge to study them.

OTHER CONTRIBUTORS

Among other contributors to the philosophical insights that go with the new rhetoric, first place must go to the movement called General Semantics. Colleagues of this persuasion such as Samuel I. Hayakawa, Alfred Korzybski, Wendell Johnson and the late Irving J. Lee, whatever be your verdict of their general thesis, have done much to awaken interest in the common blocks and misconceptions that have been crippling good communication for a long time. Hayakawa's clear and interesting style has already given thousands of students a consciousness of the pitfalls of abstrac-

---

19Burke, Kenneth, *A Rhetoric of Motives* (New York: George Braziller, Inc., 1955), p. 92.

20Notes in Burke's own typescript commenting on the first draft of this summary, Andover, New Jersey, December 22, 1956.

tion, definition and word-thought-thing relationships that was otherwise unavailable.[21] Lee's simplicity and usually clean logic in his films and books, and Johnson's healing work with aphasics indicate the basic necessity of a more healthy way of expressing ourselves founded on a sound philosophy of communication. And if the General Semanticists, in the negative aspects of their theory, have attempted to assassinate some straw men, like the syllogism and the supposed absolute identity of "is,"[22] perhaps that is a matter of the kind of well-meant misunderstanding that the new rhetoric is already on the way to alleviating.

There are many other resources at the disposal of those interested in the new rhetoric. After the works of Richards, Burke and the General Semanticists, and those of the historic masters from Aristotle to George Campbell, there are current works in abundance. Pertinent are the new psychologies, the logic of the Vienna Circle, the anthropological and sociological studies of the past fifty years, the labors of descriptive and comparative linguists, literary criticism from Coleridge to Crane and Richards and even the newer literature itself.

But in particular, the interests of rhetoric-minded teachers will be rewarded by the following works with the philosophical slant: Max Black (*Language and Philosophy*), Susanne K. Langer (*Philosophy in a New Key*), Paul Kecskemeti (*Meaning, Communication and Value*), P. Coffey (*Epistemology: or the Theory of Knowledge*), and Jacques Maritain (*The Degrees of Knowledge*). For the psychological approach useful works are: Boyd Barrett (*Motive Force and Motivation Tracks*), Charles Morris (*Signs, Language and Behavior*), Robert T. Oliver (*The Psychology of Persuasive Speech*), H. L. Hollingworth (*The Psychology of Thought*) and G. K. Zipf (*The Psychology of Language*). If there is a sociological-anthropological angle in our attitudes towards rhetoric, it might seem to be covered adequately by: Harold Innes (*Empire and Communication*), J. A. M. Meerloo (*Conversation and Communication*), Wilbur Schramm (*Communication in Modern Society*) and C. G.

---

[21]Hayakawa's *Language in Thought and Action,* originally written for use as a freshman composition text, became a Harcourt, Brace and Company bestseller in 1939.

[22]Black, Max, *Language and Philosophy* (Ithaca, New York: The Cornell University Press, 1949), pp. 239-240.

Jung (*Psyche and Symbol*). Looking at Rhetoric from the mathematical, logical and linguistic points of view are: Claude Shannon and Warren Weaver (*The Mathematical Theory of Communication*), William Empson (*The Seven Types of Ambiguity*), Paul Lazarsfeld (*Communication Research*), Susanne K. Langer (*An Introduction to Symbolic Logic*), Edward Sapir (*Language*), and Bess Sondel (*The Humanity of Words*).

BRASS TACKS

The heart of this chapter's contention is not only that we should look to a philosophy of communication, but that specifically we should incorporate certain presuppositive or philosophical inquiries immediately into the classroom rhetoric itself. Fortunately the great part of a philosophy of rhetoric or communication fits snugly under four heads which could be adopted as added chapters to our freshman communication textbooks. They are: Word-Thought-Thing Relationships; Abstraction; Definition; and Comprehension. Such studies would certainly put some muscle and flesh on the dry bones of what we have been calling composition. All the deliberations of Richards and Burke and many proposed by the General Semanticists fall under one or other of these four heads. In Aristotle's time such study was done side-by-side with rhetoric in the same curriculum. In our time, considering the urgent need we have for a full-time, universally applicable, informal-dress art of expression, it is healthy to look at all the possibilities for rhetoric. It may not be too much to hope that a deeper perusal of the insights of Richards, Burke and others may shorten the search for these happy possibilities.

chapter 4

SOME RECENT DEVELOPMENTS IN LOGIC

*Monroe Beardsley**

Taken broadly, as is appropriate in the present context, logic may be said to be concerned with the general methodological principles involved in the acquisition of knowledge. In this sense, logic encompasses a variety of studies, which are, however, usefully gathered into three groups: formal, or deductive, logic; inductive logic, or scientific methods; and semiotic, or the study of symbols (including words), and of the role they play in reasoning. Each of these three subjects has its theoretical and its applied, or practical, side. And it is applied logic — the technology of knowledge — that we draw on in teaching the reading and writing of discursive prose, skill in the organization and communication of information, the critical evaluation of argument. The composition and communication teacher is an applied logician, who looks to the logical theorist for his principles; but he does not take without giving in return, for his classroom can be a laboratory in which those principles are tested and sometimes revised.

Until recently, the logical canon, so to speak — the theoretical principles on which the applied logician could draw — seemed well-established and highly stable, though there might remain a good deal to be discovered in the pedagogy of logic. The distinction between deductive and inductive arguments, the structure of the syllogism, the logical forms of propositions, the logic of scientific explanation, the nature and rules of definition — to mention

---

*Professor of Philosophy, Swarthmore College.

some familiar examples — seemed reasonably secure. Even if these topics were poorly or misleadingly explained in some elementary logic and composition books, there were sources to which the applied logician might go for sound and accepted doctrine.

However, in recent years some interesting, and possibly revolutionary, new developments have occurred — first in philosophy and philosophical method, then, as a consequence, in logical theory itself. And it may well be that during the coming years the applied logician will find considerable help and enlightenment. The past half-century has seen a tremendous growth in the technical aspects of logical theory — for example, in mathematical logic, in the epistemological problems of induction and scientific theory-construction, and in the theory of language and meaning. This has lengthened the distance between the supply-depot of logical theory and the battleground of logical practice. But the new developments, if they continue, have the tendency to bring closer together the abstract concepts and principles of the pure logician and the daily work of the argument-appraiser.

The movement in philosophy may, for convenience, be said to have begun with the circulation, during the 1930's, of various copies of two typescripts, called the "Blue Book" and the "Brown Book" — transcripts of monologues by the late Ludwig Wittgenstein, of Cambridge University (see Bibliography, *10*). Wittgenstein's way of going at philosophy, shown more fully in his last work (see *11*), had a new and invigorating sound. One of its most significant features was an approach to philosophical problems by going back to the language of daily life, to "ordinary language," and considering, with great subtlety and sensitivity, the "logical grammar" of certain familiar words. Wittgenstein held that it is confusion about these words, and unawareness of their peculiar flexibility of use, that leads us into asking wrong questions, and that this is responsible for philosophical perplexity. And he undertook to show how this special sort of perplexity can in many cases be dissipated by a proper reconsideration of the language in which it is expressed. Out of his highly original work (here all too sketchily labelled) has come a flourishing philosophical school, variously called "Oxford analysis," "the ordinary-language school," and "therapeutic positivism" — a considerable group of able thinkers, of whom Gilbert Ryle (see *2*) is outstanding, whose methods derive from Wittgenstein and apply his guiding principles.

Among the fields in which these philosophers and their friends have begun to work fruitfully are the three fields of logic. I propose to describe, quite briefly, some of the most interesting and radical of their new proposals for revising traditionally accepted logical theory. I shall make no attempt to determine here whether, or to what extent, these proposals will stand up under criticism and should become accepted logical doctrine. Some of them may be mistaken, some of them may change the logical canon profoundly over the next decades, as they are worked out and improved. But in any case, they are worth the attention of the applied logician, who can throw light on them in his own way by seeing whether, or in what way, they can help him in his own job.

In formal logic we are concerned with necessary inference; that is, we study the conditions under which one proposition (or statement) follows necessarily from another, or from others. An inference in which the conclusion does follow necessarily is called a "valid inference." The formal logician makes a distinction between the *form* and the *content* of a proposition. Thus, for example, "No giants are gentle" and "No lambs are fierce" are said to have the same logical form, though very different contents, since one refers to giants and the other to lambs. The logical form is then abstracted and exhibited by itself as the matrix "No . . . are - - -," where the blank spaces stand for any terms that might be inserted to transform the matrix into an actual proposition. And the fundamental principle on which the logician builds is this: the validity of an inference depends solely upon the logical form of the propositions involved in it. For example, in the simplest sort of case, if the proposition "No fierce animals are lambs" can be validly inferred from the proposition "No lambs are fierce animals," this is because they both have the "No . . . are - - -" form, except that the terms are reversed.

This axiom of formal logic has been taken as basic throughout a large part of the history of logic, though not so clearly understood and formulated until our own time. If it is true, then all necessary inference, or deductive reasoning, can be reduced to rules, by means of which we can determine decisively and exactly whether any given inference is or is not valid. And this holds out great promise for the application of formal logic to practical affairs.

Yet it has always been recognized that there is a large gap between formal logic itself and the actual inferences that we encounter in the ordinary course of life — a gap that is the cause of some misery to the applied logician. The formal logician finds that in working out systematically the principles of valid inference, he does best to abandon ordinary language in favor of a symbolic system, and in this way have come about the most striking logical achievements of our century. But the newspaper and the student's theme are written in English (or something resembling English), not symbolic logic: how do we apply the rules there? Suppose we find someone saying, "Lambs never are fierce animals; therefore, there can't be any fierce animals that are lambs." These do not seem to have the same logical form at all, when we drop out the terms, yet the inference seems intuitively to be sound. Does that mean that validity does not depend on logical form after all?

The standard reply of the formal logician is, of course, that logical form may be disguised by grammatical form. The proposition "Lambs never are fierce animals" has the same logical form as "No lambs are fierce animals;" and the proposition "There aren't any fierce animals that are lambs" has the same logical form as "No fierce animals are lambs." So that, while it did not at first seem so, it was in fact the underlying logical form that guaranteed the validity of the inference. But here we have an important new principle: grammatically different propositions may have an identical logical form. And since it is the form that determines the capacity of a proposition to yield inferences or to be inferred from others, it is important that we recognize logical form, if we are interested in clear reasoning, and clear writing. So the student is taught to examine sentences in ordinary language and classify them according to logical form, and to rewrite some of them in *standard forms* (like "No lambs are fierce") designed to make the underlying form wholly explicit. And he is given practice in testing at least simple deductive arguments, of a syllogistic form, by the appropriate rules.

It is at this point, however, that the applied logician is apt to run into difficulties with his students. First, the formal logician is interested in generality; when he lumps together grammatically different expressions as examples of the same logical form, he is content to ignore differences of meaning that are of great importance to the flexible use of English. Consider: (a) "I'll go,

provided you go," (b) "On the assumption that you'll go, I promise to go, too," and (c) "If you'll go, I will:" these are all taken
as the same conditional proposition, whose standard form is "If
you will go, then I will go." He may admit that they differ in
meaning, but he says their essential meaning, or logical force, is
extractable and restatable in the "If . . . then" form. And indeed,
some applied logicians have trained their students to confine themselves to a sort of antiseptic logical baby-talk, in which words like
"except," "unless," "only," "provided," have disappeared, to make
way for "all," "some," "no," "if . . . then," and a few others.

Second, in ordinary English we make many inferences that
don't seem to be reducible to logical form: "This is blue, therefore
it is colored," or "She called him her uncle, so he must be male."
What is the applied logician to do with these? The prevailing
theory is that if they are valid, it must be because of their implicit
logical form, however hidden or submerged, but the composition
teacher and his students may well be puzzled about this. It is
much easier to see that these inferences are valid than to figure out
their logical form.

Now the whole conception of logical form and its relation to
inferences in ordinary language has been challenged by P. F. Strawson (see 6, esp. ch. 2). He holds that it is a mistake to say that
all necessary inference is formal. The logical theorist can, of course,
construct a logical system (either of symbols or of selected English
words) in which all permissible inferences are specified in formal
rules. But it is a serious, though widespread, error (he thinks)
to say that ordinary language consists of, or implicitly contains,
or should be changed over into, such a system. We need not be
puzzled to discover what rules we are going by in inferring that
something is colored because it is blue, or male because it is an
uncle — the fact is that to reason this way is not to follow any
formal rule. Not that there are no rules in ordinary language —
some inferences, like "No A are B, therefore no B are A," do fall
into a class of inferences about which we can state a general rule.
But other equally necessary inferences do not, according to Strawson.

If the principle that all necessary inference goes by formal
rules is wrong, then it would of course greatly ease the practical
logician's task, and it might indeed redirect some of his teaching
to a rather different goal. It might still be helpful to see what
formal rules we do use in some inferences, and how these rules are

best formulated; but in other cases we would simply have to acknowledge that there are no such rules — though there is still a distinction between valid and invalid inferences. And then students, instead of giving up "except" and "provided" for simpler and more direct expressions, should come to learn how to use them better, and exploit their subtly different meanings.

I suppose that nothing has appeared to be more firmly settled as a part of logical theory, since the beginning of the subject, than the doctrine of the syllogism. The applied logician now knows, better than Aristotle, that it is not to be taken as the whole, or major part, of formal logic, but he still finds it a useful example of clear reasoning, and it does seem possible to find innumerable examples of argument from daily life, editorials, and Supreme Court decisions, whose validity or invalidity yields to explanation by the principles of syllogistic reasoning.

But an interesting and original criticism of the doctrine of the syllogism has been made by Stephen Toulmin (see 7, chs. 3, 4). Toulmin has proposed a new "layout," as he calls it, of arguments, distinguishing (1) the conclusion, (2) the data advanced to support it, (3) the warrant for saying that the data support the conclusion, (4) the backing of the warrant, and (5), in some cases, the "rebuttal," which guards against circumstances under which the warrant may not be applicable. Thus in the classic example, the conclusion is "Socrates is mortal," and the datum is "Socrates is a man." The warrant is a rule, "If someone is a man then he may (certainly) be taken to be mortal." The backing of the warrant is that "All men so far observed have died." Toulmin objects to the traditional form because it fails to make evident this distinction between the warrant and its backing — both are ambiguously lumped together as the major premise, "All men are mortal." The formal logician, he argues, has set up an artificial ideal, or model, of argument, which obscures important differences between various kinds of argument.

Thus Toulmin believes that his layout is broad enough to accommodate various types of argument, and bring out the differences in standards or kinds of evidence that will be acceptable in various fields, in mathematics, law, art criticism, physics, or history. Moreover, the traditional distinction between deductive and inductive arguments would be replaced by a number of distinctions that are, he thinks, confused together in it: for example, the distinction between arguments that use, and those that establish, warrants.

Working along other, but comparable, lines, Michael Scriven has made a thoroughgoing reexamination of the concept of explanation, in the scientific sense (see 5). According to the standard view, explanation is a particular logical relation between a proposition, or set of propositions, E, and a fact, or set of facts, F. We would say, for example, that the proposition that a given baseball club was weak in pitching (E) explains why it did not win the pennant (F). But what is this peculiar logical relation? First, it seems that in this example the weak pitching explains the loss of the pennant because it makes (or helps to make) that loss understandable: it leads us to find the loss less surprising than it appeared before we explained it. If we had known how weak the pitching was, then we might have been able (it seems) to predict the loss with some confidence, as no doubt it was in fact predicted by some sports experts. Second, it seems that the two things, E and F, must therefore be connected by some kind of generalization or law, according to which F is to be expected from E because the truth of F can be deduced from E by means of that law. The inference might then be roughly set up as follows:

> The Yankees have a weak pitching staff (E)
> Clubs with weak pitching staffs always fail to win pennants (G)
> _____
> The Yankees lost the pennant (F)

(where the horizontal line asserts that the proposition below it follows necessarily from those above). We start out by knowing F, which is what we wish to explain; E explains it because if E is true, then F necessarily follows (assuming the generalization G).

This reasoning exemplifies the so-called "deductive model" of explanation: the explanation-relation is identified with a necessary logical connection. And it is this widely-accepted model that Scriven attacks.

He argues first that the generalization G should not be called a part of the explanation. Besides the explanation E itself, one may be called upon to produce various subordinate defenses, which he calls truth-justifying grounds (support for the truth of the statement that the pitching staff was weak), role-justifying grounds (support for the claim that in fact the weakness of its pitching staff is capable of causing a club to fail to win the pennant), and type-justifying grounds (support for the assumption that this *sort* of explanation is called for in this context, rather than, say, a physiological or economic one — injuries, or a penurious owner). All three sorts of support might become suitable if the explanation is challenged, but no one is more central, Scriven holds, than the others.

His chief criticism, however, is directed against the deductive model itself, and he makes a number of points. The most important is his questioning whether the generalization G is necessary or available for explanations — at least explanations of the same sort as the example, that is, historical explanations. Any teacher of logic who has tried to explain the standard account of explanation must have encountered problems. Consider the example again. Is G really true? Surely not, as it stands, Scriven argues. We could say, to be safe, "*Most* clubs with weak pitching staffs fail to win," and perhaps this would be true — but then F can no longer be deduced from E (the argument would have an undistributed middle). Perhaps we can keep the "Always," if we add qualifications — "provided the other clubs in the league have strong staffs, and provided the Yankee hitters are not outstandingly good, and provided the other clubs do not suffer a great many injuries . . ." etc. But if we do this, we are in danger of transforming G into something like a tautology: "It will lose if it's poor enough to make it lose." And this is hardly informative, or helpful to the explanation.

One of the purposes of Scriven's argument is to remove the puzzle that plagues the applied logician here. According to his view, the mediating proposition (the one that connects E and F) is not a generalization at all, but a special sort of proposition, a "truism," which states that something is normally, or typically, or characteristically the case, in such a way as to admit exceptions, but only if they are backed up by unusual circumstances. Explanation is therefore, he holds, not deductive at all. Nor should it be confused with prediction: the fact that we can explain the loss of the pennant after it has happened does not in any way require us to have been able to predict it before it happened. Predictions in such matters are notoriously fallible, and if we think of all explanations as predictions after the fact (predictions backward in time), then we will wonder how they can be anything but very risky. But once the pennant is lost, we are in a position to look among a relatively small number of factors that we know from past experience could have been the cause, and we can in many cases effectively eliminate all but one, and come up with a fairly conclusive result.

If Scriven's view is right (and there is much more to it than can be indicated here), then it will no longer be required of the practical logician to try to force every explanation into the deductive pattern. Moreover, it will turn his attention into lines of inquiry that have been precluded or minimized — not "What laws, or generalizations, does the historian use?" (if he actually uses none), but "How does he know what explanatory possibilities to consider, and choose the best among them?"

One other development has to do with meaning and the definition of terms. According to the prevailing view, when a term is limited to one of its senses, it designates certain properties that are individually the necessary, and collectively the sufficient, conditions for applying the term. Thus the term "husband" can be precisely defined as "man who is married," for it may be correctly applied to all objects that are (a) human, (b) male, and (c) married — and only to those objects. It is customary for textbooks on logic, then, to lay down the rule that in constructing a definition of any term "X" we must include in the defining term (or *definiens*) only properties that *all* X's have — the necessary conditions for being an X. Now with a family-relation term like "husband," and with simple geometrical terms also frequently used for illustration, this rule is easy to apply. But teachers and their students have often been troubled about applying the rule to many quite ordinary words: "house," "chair," "newspaper," "watch." When we ask what properties a watch *has* to have, we can be quite skeptical, if we press the question: couldn't we call it a watch even if it is not metal, has no dial or hands (but some alternative method of showing time), weighs half a pound, etc.? Even if we insist in the end on certain absolutely indispensable properties, such as that it must have moving parts, these will not by any means be sufficient to distinguish watches from other things.

Recently there has been questioning of this traditional view that the properties of things like watches can be divided neatly into necessary ones and contingent ones, and whether the rule of defini-

tion that gives so much trouble might in fact be wrong.   Perhaps
we are trying to take ordinary terms in a way that misrepresents
them, and this is what causes the trouble.   It was Wittgenstein
(see *10*, p. 17, and *11*, Part I, sections 65ff) who suggested that
terms like "game" might not carve out a class of things that have
some specific set of common properties, but rather a "family" of
things, each of which resembles some of the others in one way
or another.   The "open texture" of empirical terms has been discussed by a number of other writers (see *9*; *8*, ch. 6, §2; *1*, chs.
5, 11).   And Wittgenstein's suggestion has been further developed
by Michael Scriven, who has proposed a fundamental overhauling of
the traditional distinctions (see *3* and *4*).   To ask for the necessary
and sufficient conditions of being a game (or a watch, or an apple,
or a case of scarlet fever), in the ordinary sense, may be to ask for
something that does not exist.   We can explain the meanings of
these terms in two ways.   We can give examples, of course.   And
we can give a list of *criteria.*   Thus, though a watch doesn't have
to have moving hands, still the presence of moving hands in a
small metal object will count as evidence that it is a watch, will
help us recognize it as such.   So we would want to mention the
hands in explaining the meaning of the term, even if we do not
want to list them as a necessary condition.

Scriven's proposal would explain, and help the logician to
accept, a fact that has long irked him — the extent to which dic-
tionary-definitions use words like "usually" in mentioning properties.   The "logic of criteria" seems to have capabilities of interesting
development.   Some problems about it remain.   But if these are
overcome, it will require a revision of the traditional doctrine of
definition, and this revision will bring that account closer to ordinary language.   It will be less simple than the present one, but on
the other hand it will apply more directly and with less strain to
familiar words.   Instead of insisting that the student divide all the
properties of watches — those that belong in the defining term
and those that do not — we might ask for a threefold distinction:
(1) having some changing indication of time is a necessary property; (2) having a small dial with numbers is not necessary, but
is one of the properties that, when it is present, helps make an
object a watch, and so it is a criterion of watchness, so to speak;
but (3) being made of gold, or by a particular manufacturer, is a
purely contingent, or accidental, property.   The definition of

"watch," then, might have to be put in a form like this: "A watch is an artificial object that tells time (necessary condition) and has some of the following (criterial) properties: it is light and small enough to be conveniently carried on the person, it has a dial and moving hands or a gauge with changing numbers, it has a spring motor that is either wound up or self-winding," etc.

#

These are some of the ways in which contemporary logicians have proposed to improve existing logical theory, and what they have in common is the recognition of the great complexity of ordinary language. Perhaps the traditional principles of logic, though still applicable, apply more narrowly than has been thought, and new and more subtle principles are needed to supplement them.

Bibliography

1. Pap, Arthur. *Semantics and Necessary Truth,* New Haven: Yale University Press, 1958.
2. Ryle, Gilbert. *The Concept of Mind,* N.Y.: Barnes and Noble, 1949.
3. Scriven, Michael. "Definitions, Explanations, and Theories," in Herbert Feigl, Michael Scriven, and Grover Maxwell, eds., *Minnesota Studies in the Philosophy of Science,* Vol. II: Concepts, Theories, and the Mind-Body Problem, Minneapolis: University of Minnesota Press, 1958.
4. Scriven, Michael. "The Logic of Criteria," *Journal of Philosophy,* LVI (1959): 857-68.
5. Scriven, Michael. "Truisms as the Grounds for Historical Explanations," in Patrick Gardiner, ed., *Theories of History,* Glencoe, Ill.: Free Press, 1959.
6. Strawson, P. F. *Introduction to Logical Theory,* London: Methuen, N.Y.: Wiley, 1952.
7. Toulmin, Stephen. *The Uses of Argument,* Cambridge: Cambridge University Press, 1958.
8. von Wright, George Henrik, *A Treatise on Induction and Probability,* London: Routledge and Kegan Paul, 1951.
9. Waismann, Friedrich. "Verifiability," in *Proceedings of the Aristotelian Society,* Supplementary vol. XIX, London, 1945.
10. Wittgenstein, Ludwig. *The Blue and Brown Books,* Oxford: Blackwell, 1958.
11. Wittgenstein, Ludwig. *Philosophical Investigations,* trans. G. E. M. Anscombe, Oxford: Blackwell, 1953.

chapter 5

LINGUISTICS (English verb grammar)

*W. F. Twaddell**

Linguistics is the specialized study of the mechanisms whereby meaningful communication takes place in a social context. It is thus the reverse of our normal social behavior: usually we are concerned to express and perceive MEANINGS as the content of communication and to disregard the MECHANISMS. The linguist concentrates on the structural relations of the mechanisms for conveying meanings in a language rather than on the meanings themselves. His concern is for the habits rather than the choices, the compulsory rather than the optional distinctions, the forms rather than the contents, the general code rather than the particular messages.

There are rigorous and intricate procedures for analyzing the code structure of a language, on all levels. Pronunciation, as the most habitual aspect, least susceptible to individual choice, is the most fully analyzed object of linguistic study. There are techniques for an objective, economical, and complete description of the pronunciation of a language, including the "vowels and consonants" and the significant features of relative loudness, melody, rhythm, and timing, which are semantically and grammatically important, notably so in English.

In a grammatical description, a linguist makes his classifications on a formal, not a semantic, basis. He does not start from an a priori system of expected grammatical categories (like "future,

---

*Professor of Linguistics and German, Brown University.

subjunctive, indirect object, active, plural, feminine, predicate nom-
inative") and then try to find the mechanisms to convey those
meanings.   Instead, he observes the actually occurrent constructions and classifies them into a system of partial similarities and
partial differences among the forms as they actually exist.   Only
then does he look for semantic features which may correlate, wholly
or partly, with the observed features of grammatical form.

The remainder of this chapter is a specimen of such linguistic
analysis of certain grammatical phenomena with which its readers
are familiar as a part (perhaps unconscious) of their own linguistic
and grammatical behavior: the English verb construction in the
unaffected usage of adult educated Americans.   It is a summary —
in part a reformulation — of many technical studies and books
by a dozen or so linguists during the past two decades.   No attempt
is made here to supply bibliographical references or attribute credits
or discuss disagreements: a professional linguist will recognize the
originator of a particular formulation, and other readers should
not be distracted.

0.   English verb grammar employs inflection to a slight degree (3rd-singular -s; past -ed or stem alternation), but is chiefly a
system of compound constructions with auxiliaries and verbal
adjuncts.

1.0 There are two sets of auxiliaries, primary and modal.
The primary auxiliaries are *be* (be; am, is, are, was, were; being;
been); *have* (have; have, has, had; having); *do* (do, does, did).
The modal auxiliaries are *can, could, dare, may, might, must, need,
ought, shall, should, will, would.*   The primary set is formally
characterized by an inflectional 3rd-singular -s, the modal set by
the lack of this inflection.   In expanded constructions containing
members of both primary and modal sets, the modal auxiliary
precedes the primary auxiliary, never vice versa.[1]

---

[1]Some auxiliaries are paralleled in the lexicon by true full verbs: *Be* in the
rare meaning "exist" and as a constituent of verb phrases like "be careful"; the
copula *be* is best treated in a different category: see footnote 2, p. 52. *Have* =
"possess, participate in a relationship (have a brother, have a cold, have a
vacation)". *Do* = "perform, practice regularly" etc. *Dare* in several transitive
and intransitive meanings. *Need* = "require."   *Will* = "choose; bequeath."
Of these true verbs, only *be* in American usage, *be* and *have* in British usage,
behave differently from other true verbs with respect to co-occurrence with *do* and
its inflections in negation, questions, emphasis, and repetition.

1.2. A phonological feature of the auxiliaries is reduction to unstressed forms, except for the sub-group *dare, may, might, need, ought.*

1.3. General formal grammatical characteristics of the auxiliaries are:

(1) Occurrence before unstressed -n't; rare with *may, might, shall;* lacking with *am.*

(2) Occurrence before the subject in questions except when the subject is itself the interrogative element ("Who . . .?   What . . . ?   Which [noun] . . .?").   In the more formal written styles and in platform style, an auxiliary also precedes the subject after sentence-initial elements with negative or quasi-negative meanings. ("Not only is she living beyond her means . . . .   Scarcely had he arrived when . . . .   Seldom will we find . . . .   Never have I heard such a story . . . .   Nowhere else do we encounter . . . .   Neither do I.   Only in the classics can you . . . .") — "Conditional inversion," the word order with initial auxiliary followed by subject as a substitute for "if", is now restricted to the formal styles, and there it rarely occurs except in the formula *"Had"* + subject + past participle.

(3a) A pattern of grammatical stress and pitch signals.   When the utterance is "insistent" — i.e. when there is a contrast between affirmation and negation — the signal for "emphasis of insistence" is that the chief stress of the phrase is upon the auxiliary.   ("No, I cán't work at that desk.   He wás bitten by an alligator, whatever he may have told you.   But we háve done everything you told us to.")

(3b) When there is "emphasis of contrast" between the auxiliary itself and another auxiliary or adjunct or true verb, the contrasted auxiliary has not only the chief stress but also the extrahigh pitch.   ("We COULD stay, but we'd [=would] rather not. That MIGHT work, but I don't think it will.")   Not all speakers distinguish between the emphases of insistence and contrast in this way; for some the extra-high pitch is stylistic rather than grammatical.

(4) The auxiliary of a construction serves as a substitute for the entire construction in an immediately following second occurrence, including answers ("She can drive better than he can.   I'll be working there, and I understand that you will too.   Have you been living here long?   Yes, we have.   Is it lying there?   No, it

isn't. Ethel was admitted, but Tom wasn't. The flora usually changes as the climate does.") See also Footnote 7, p. 61.

1.4.1. The four grammatical characteristics of auxiliaries are thus: -n't; position before subject in questions; as bearer of stress and/or pitch for "emphasis"; as substitute in repetition. Not only do the auxiliaries have the privilege of occurrence in these functions; they are indispensable in English grammar. Hence when a construction is negative, interrogative, "emphatic", or repeated, there must be an auxiliary. But the corresponding affirmative, declarative, "non-emphatic" sentence may lack an auxiliary. ("He teaches Latin. They lived in Cleveland.") To construct the corresponding negative, interrogative, or insistent sentence, or to provide for a substitute in a repetition, the purely grammatical requirement of an auxiliary is satisfied by the empty auxiliary *do* (*do, does, did*); *do* precedes -n't, precedes the subject in questions, bears the stress for insistence, and replaces a full verb in repetition. *Do* has no semantic content whatever. It is the -n't which negates, the auxiliary-subject sequence which inquires, the stress which insists, and mere fact of being an auxiliary which substitutes for a verb. These are not four separate grammatical functions of the auxiliary *do; do* has the one single function of filling a position in a construction which must be filled by an auxiliary, when there is no other auxiliary to do so.

1.4.2. The set of primary auxiliaries is thus simplified by relegating *do* to the purely automatic, predictable, semantically null status of the empty auxiliary in negation, interrogation, insistence, and repetition.[2]

2.0. The primary set of auxiliaries then consists of *be* and *have*. In the paradigm which follows, inflectional forms of *be* will be represented by *is/was, being, been;* inflectional forms of *have* by *has/had*.

---

[2]Similarly, the copula *be* is the empty verb: it functions merely to fill the requirements of a sentence for a verb when there is no semantic content requiring any lexical verb. It follows or precedes a subject as required, in the proper place for a verb; it performs (elaborately!) the functions of subject-agreement; it bears negation; it bears the stress of emphasis; it displays the "Past" inflections; it replaces a verb with -ing or in the infinitive or past participle form in constructions otherwise lacking a lexical verb. Beyond these purely grammatical functions, the copula *be* has precisely no meaning.

2.1. These two auxiliaries are linked with inflection for "Past" to constitute the primary verb grammar of English. The inner category of verb constructions consists of four Modifications.

I.   "Past" (-ed, alternate form of stem)
II.   "Current relevance" (*have* + Past participle)
III.   "Limited duration" (*be* + -ing)
IV.   "Passive" (*be* + Past participle)

There may be semantic restrictions with a particular lexical verb, but there is no grammatical limitation upon co-occurrence of these four modifications.   Given a lexical verb of sufficient semantic versatility, all of the sixteen possible combinations exist, although some are infrequent.   The full paradigm for the four modifications is thus:

—	eats	II, III	has been eating
I	ate	II, IV	has been eaten
II	has eaten	III, IV	is being eaten
III	is eating	I, II, III	had been eating
IV	is eaten	I, II, IV	had been eaten
I, II	had eaten	I, III, IV	was being eaten
I, III	was eating	II, III, IV	has been being eaten
I, IV	was eaten	I, II, III, IV	had been being eaten

2.2. The formal order of combining the four modifications is given by the sequence of their roman-numeral indices.   If the "Past" Modification (I) is involved, it appears as suffix or stem alternation at the beginning of the construction ("ate, was eating, had eaten," etc.).   *Have* (+ past participle) precedes *be* if both are involved in a construction.   The *be* auxiliary appears as *been* after *have*, as *being* after *be*.   The first auxiliary in a construction bears the "Past" modification if I is involved; otherwise it bears the subject-agreement marker -s or —.[3]

3.0. The semantics of the four modifications notoriously is one of the most intricate topics of English grammar.   The traditional labels are not satisfactory guides to meaning, and the inter-

---

[3]If the first auxiliary is *be*, the subject-agreement marking is elaborate: [I] *am* / [3rd singular] *is* / [plural] *are*; with Modification I,]singular] *was* / [plural] *were*.

action of the meanings of lexical verbs with the grammatical meanings of the modifications has complicated the analysis. The following analysis observes two principles of caution: (1) the absence of
any one of the four modifications does not necessarily signal a denial of the meaning of the modification; (2) a particular modification need not have a unique meaning, but may have different
semantic functions with various semantically different classes of
lexical verbs.

3.1.1. Modification I, "Past" (-ed, alternative form of stem).
This can be labelled "past" with some reservations. Primarily its
grammatical meaning is "earlier-ness", reference to a time anterior
to the report and only to such time.

3.1.2. Note that the lack of Modification I in no way denies
earlierness. A sentence like "He eats peas with his knife" factually
refers to past and presumptively to future time. Only a pea-eater
with a past rcord of knife-using can be referred to thus. Similarly
with all verb constructions lacking any of the Modifications (what
is traditionally called the "present tense"); that absence of modification ("eats" etc.) signals nothing at all in terms of time; nothing beyond the semantic content of the lexical verb itself is conveyed;
nothing is implied as to chronology: the construction is totally
descriptive and not narrative.

3.1.3. Stage directions and the derivative usages in the "present tense" illustrate the timelessness of constructions without modification. The direction "Bertha enters and picks up a glove" refers
to all times when a particular segment of a performance occurs.
The demonstration formula ("I pour the contents of this flask
into the mixture and then I stir for thirty seconds") signals a
ritual, an indefinitely repeatable performance. The unmodified
verb construction in newspaper headlines is of the nature of a stage
direction or topical index in relation to the narrative of the story
itself. ("White Sox clinch pennant. Asian nations disagree on
fallout survey. House upholds veto. Thermometer skids to 15°.")
Likewise, a construction without modification ("eats," etc.) is
available for earlier-time signalling in the "historical present" which
converts a chronicle into a recitation, indicating the timelessness of
the events as story or plot no longer time-bound as an individually
observed or remembered sequence.

3.1.4. Thus, the construction without modification ("eats,
arrives," etc.) is versatile in combining with associated time-clues.

It is the usual companion of future time-clues, whether adverbial ("I leave at 4:10 tomorrow") or contextual ("The first class meets in Room 107") or situational ("You transfer to Flight 208 at Omaha" uttered in Denver). The construction with Modification III (*be* + ing) shares this availability for future-time signalling; see 3.3.1. below.

3.1.5. Modification I has the primary meaning of restricting the reference to chronologically earlier time. But there are two important secondary usages in which earlierness is not signalled:

a. "Sequence of tenses": the automatic predictable occurrence of I in verb constructions which are syntactically dependent upon a I construction. ("You said you had eaten. I thought they were studying. She wanted you to know that she saw us.")

b. "Unreal conditional." Some conditional sentences occur with "if" without any meaning of unreality. "If they come, we talk to them" is unmodified, hence timeless. A simple conditional which is the Past parallel has Modification I in both clauses "if they came, we talked to them." But when the "if" + Modification I is associated with another construction containing *could, might, should, would,* then the Modification I has no chronological reference, but instead signals unreality. ("If they came, we would [might, should, could] talk to them.") The reference in this construction is grammatically timeless; usually it applies to future time because of the practical fact that conditional unreality is usually a property of the future rather than the past. The signalling of past unreality, "contrary-to-fact," is via a combination of Modifications I and II, one with "if" and the other with *could, might, should, would.* ("If they had come, we would have talked to them.")[4]

3.2.0. Modification II. *Have* + past participle. This is the modification traditionally and unhelpfully called "perfect." Its contribution to the meaning of a construction is suggested, inadequately but not misleadingly, by the label "Current relevance." It signals the persistence of results, and continued validity, up through the time of the report. Contrast the meanings in

---

[4]The auxiliary *be* after "if" has its usual subject-agreement inflection in simple conditional constructions, whether timeless or Past. ("If he is available, I'll talk to him. If he was available, I talked to him. If they were available, I talked to them.") But in the unreal constructions, the *was/were* distinction is eliminated in standard English: "If he were here, I would talk to him."

— Alligators bite him
III   An alligator is biting him.
I   An alligator bit him
II   An alligator has bitten him.

As between the last two examples, "has bitten" contributes a meaning of current relevance compatible with "and he is furious" or "and he is bleeding and needs help" or "but it isn't fatal." The "bit" (Modification I only) by no means denies current relevance; it merely does not assert it.

3.2.1. It is the function of Modification II to convey a continuation of pertinent effects up to the present. The quantitative chronology is not grammatically significant. "I ate breakfast two hours ago" does not by its grammar imply anything as to current hunger or satiety; but "I've been in Vermont" does grammatically signal the current biographical relevance of the visit, a relevance not denied by "I was in Vermont." Some suggestive pairs:

"His parents spoiled him.   His parents have spoiled him."
"The wire was broken.   The wire has been broken."
"He was being questioned.   He had been being questioned."
"The evidence disappeared.   The evidence has disappeared."

3.2.2. In the logic of chronology and persistence of effects, *have* + past participle constructions are likely to have a reference to the recent past; but this is a practical, not a grammatical, feature. Compare "God created man in His own image" and "God has created man in His own image." The Modifications II and I are thus distinguished semantically in the explicit specification of the current relevance of earlier events. *Have* + past participle links past event and present situation. It certainly does not deny pastness, nor does it necessarily mean "completed action" in the sense of implying a lack of further continuation or repetition; if such an implication is to be conveyed, it is via the "emphasis" signal (main stress, extra-high pitch) with a following contrastive element. ("We háve thought of adopting your proposal but we don't see our way clear at this time. Jo wás here this morning, but she hasn't been back since lunch. He díd plan to go to Florida but changed his mind.") The meaning past-but-not-present via stress on the auxiliary háve paraphrases "It is true that . . . ." and thus preserves the ingredient of current relevance.

3.2.3. For a positive non-contrastive expression of a break in continuation, the adjunct "used to" is available. ("Edith used to live here. He used to go to Florida in the winter.")

3.3.0. Modification III. *Be* + -*ing*. This is traditionally called "progressive," a label as bad as "perfect" for the purposes of describing English grammar. Modification III is the most versatile of the four. Its semantic contribution varies according to the semantic content of the lexical verb, and there are some lexical verbs whose semantic content is almost immune to the *be* + -*ing* modification. In the listing above, in 2.1., Modification III was characterized as signalling limited duration. It is a peculiarity of this modification that it can signal either the limitation or the duration or both, depending on the semantics of the lexical verb in the construction.

3.3.1. Lexical verbs whose semantic content is inherently of a durational nature ("reside, compose, plan, pour, hunt, eat, sit") may participate in a *be* + -*ing* construction; the meaning is then "limitation of the duration." ("Where are you living? She's writing her dissertation. What was he hunting for? They had been eating mushrooms.") The contrast between lack of modification and Modification III with such durative lexical verbs appears in "Miss Thompson teaches French, but this summer she is studying Russian" or "Usually our graduate students teach two sections, but this semester several of them are teaching three sections;" compare "Usually our graduate students are teaching at this hour."[5]

3.3.2. Other lexical verbs have an inherent semantic content of limitation-of-duration ("break, find, hit, call = give a name to, recommend, discharge, stumble"). With such verbs, Modification III specifically adds duration, often in the form of iteration:

"Are you finding any mushrooms? She was hitting him with a slipper. Mack has been hitting better."

3.3.3. Some lexical verbs have meanings which are neutral with respect to duration ("turn, operate, view, provide, expect, approach"). They appear with Modification III in its full mean-

---

[5]This feature of limitation of duration makes constructions with *be* + -*ing* the closest approximation to a present tense in English, either alone or with the Passive Modification, provided the context does not contradict. Of course, with some contextual future clue, Modification III can refer to a limited future duration: "We're flying over on a jet" says the hostess in her living room in Keokuk.

ing of limitation and duration. ("They are providing free lunches this year. Were you expecting anybody? We were turning in the driveway.") [6]

3.3.4.1. A fourth semantic class of lexical verbs have meanings which inherently imply unlimited, permanent duration. This implication may be objective and logical ("resemble, know, contain, equal,") or arbitrary in English idiomatic usage ("border, possess, dislike, have a cold"). Such lexical verbs are rarely found with the *be* + -ing modification, which would be incompatible with the meaning of unlimited duration. Hence we do not find constructions like "*was resembling. *Three and five are equalling eight. *Canada is bordering on the United States." Only when an associated sentence-element enforces a limitation do we find such verbs with Modification III, for example with "more and more": "Every year American cars are resembling each other more and more."

3.3.4.2. The same semantic feature of inherently unlimited duration affects the grammar of these verbs in references to future time. (It will be recalled that most lexical verbs appear without modification or with Modification III for future reference, in association with adverbial or contextual or situational clues: see 3.1.4.; 3.3.1. above.) But the verbs under discussion do not have this property; we do not find "*The child resembles his father pretty soon. *Graustark borders on Ruritania after the treaty is signed next month. *You have a bad cold if you don't get out of those wet clothes." The implicit unlimited-duration of these lexical verbs is incompatible with the meaning "only future." To signal that "only-future" meaning, these verbs require the overt signal, the modal auxiliary *will*.

3.3.4.3. Verb + complement idioms are often arbitrary with respect to limited vs. unlimited duration. E.g. "have a cold" is idiomatically permanent ("I have a cold") but "have a good time" is arbitrarily impermanent and hence susceptible to the *be* + -ing modification: "We're having a good time, a miserable vacation."

---

[6] All three kinds of lexical verbs mentioned above regularly appear in narration or proclamation in combination with Past and Limited-duration Modifications (I and III); the meaning is then simultaneity. ("They were playing chess when the earthquake occurred. She was pulling the trigger when . . . . The rocket was approaching Venus and suddenly . . . .") In stage directions, Modification III alone signals simultaneity: "Muriel is pacing impatiently as Archibald enters." Simultaneity is logically of limited duration, hence is appropriately signalled by the *be* + -ing modification.

3.3.5.0. The reverse semantic feature — unrepeatable occurrence = inherently limited duration without possibility of iteration — of course has the same incompatibility with the *be* + -ing modification.

3.3.5.1. Lexical verb contexts with the inherent meaning of "unique event" fall in this class. ("I pronounce you man and wife. I sentence you to be . . . . This stew tastes wonderful. The doctor prescribed pelagoselenacin.") "Unique event" verbs can occur with *be* + -ing in the past simultaneity meaning. ("The preacher was pronouncing . . . when . . . . The judge was sentencing . . . and then . . . .")

3.3.5.2. With different subjects, a given predicate may mean either "unlimited permanent duration" or "unrepeatable occurrence" and be in either case normally incompatible with Modification III. ("Everything about trolley cars interests him. What you've just told me interests me greatly. — Pelagoselenacin makes her sick. What you've just told me makes me sick.")

3.3.6. The versatility of the *be* + -ing modification permits a semantic versatility in many lexical verbs, e.g. "cover" as an unlimited-duration verb with inanimate subject ("Forests covered the continent") and as a limited-duration verb with animate actor subject: ("We are covering the flower beds next week"); "think = be of the opinion" and "think = perform intellectual activity."

3.4.0. Modification IV. *Be* + past participle. This is the Passive modification. The standard term and the traditional semantic characterizations are fairly satisfactory: with the Passive modification, the subject referent undergoes an action or effect, rather than producing or constituting an action or state.

3.4.1. It is important to note that here too the absence of the modification does not necessarily deny the meaning. Thus the semantics of passive meaning can be conveyed without the overt Passive modification, i.e. in what would traditionally be called a construction in the "active voice." ("This sweater buttons up the back. The car is steering better now. The chair blew off the porch. This material doesn't wash very well.") The so-called "active infinitive with passive meaning" is familiar: "The car is delivered ready to drive. The stew wasn't fit to eat."

3.4.2. Just as some verbs are inherently incompatible with the *be* + -ing modification, some verbs rarely or never occur with the Passive modification. These are, roughly, the "intransitive"

verbs — those not found with an object complement. But the two
criteria (non-occurrence with the Passive modification, non-
occurrence with an object complement) do not wholly coincide.
The true verb "have" regularly occurs with an object, but expected
corresponding sentences with passive modification do not occur.
("*Two brothers are had by him.   *This is the worst cold that
was ever had by me.")   By idiomatic usage, "A good time was had
by all" has a borderline status beside "Everybody had a good time."

3.5. In summary: The Primary verb grammar consists of
four modifications, with proximately definable meanings.   The
absence of a particular modification in a construction does not
signal a denial of its meaning.   The presence of one, two, three,
or four modifications signals ONLY the positive semantic contri-
bution(s) of the occurrent modification(s), with no implications
beyond that.   Each of the modifications, if regarded as one term
of a binary relation, is the Yes of a Yes-or-Maybe alternative, not
of a Yes-or-No alternative.   E.g. a non-conditional construction
with only the Past Modification (I) specifically asserts earlierness,
but asserts nothing one way or the other about current relevance,
limited duration, or "passive-vs-active."   And a construction without the Past Modification in no way denies earlierness.

3.6. Since all four modifications are potentially co-occurrent
in a construction, their meanings must also be potentially compatible.   Hence their meanings CANNOT belong to one semantic
category; they CANNOT be a tense system, or an aspect system,
or a mood system, or a voice system.

The Modal Auxiliaries

4.0. These are: *can, could, dare, may, might, must, need,
ought, shall, should, will, would.*   They occur before the base (infinitive) form of a lexical verb or of the (first) auxiliary of a
construction involving one or more of Modifications II, III, IV.
The modal auxiliaries lack subject agreement.   Unlike the primary
auxiliaries, the modals do not co-occur with each other.

4.1.0. There are four pairs of modal auxiliaries, and four
unpaired ones:

can	may	shall	will				
could	might	should	would	dare	must	need	ought

4.1.1. Of the four paired auxiliaries, only *can/could* displays
complete Past Modification: *could* signals earlierness as compared

with *can*, appears in sequence of tenses, and as an unreal conditional. *May/might, shall/should, will/would* display the functions of sequence of tenses and unreal conditionals, but do not signal earlierness. That function is performed by suppletion from the set of verb adjuncts and expanded constructions, or by the use of following Modification II, *have* + past participle.[7]

4.1.2. The four unpaired modal auxiliaries, *dare, must, need, ought,* lack any form with overt Past modification. For sequence of tenses they may function without suffix or stem-alternation in the negative ("He said that we [dare not, mustn't, needn't oughtn't] stay here any longer"). Otherwise, they require suppletion for the functions of earlierness, (affirmative) sequence of tenses, and unreal conditional.

4.2. The positive semantics of the modals belongs more to lexicography than to grammar, once we have noted the relationships described above, 4.1.1-2.

4.3. The unreal-condition rôle of *could, might, should, would* has already been mentioned in 3.1.5. These forms also occur in constructions without any associated "if"-clause: "Could you get there by seven? We might be able to make it. You really should. Would you like to have me draw you a map?" Three of these signal a lesser degree of probability or urgency: *could* (*can*), *might* (*may*), *should* (*shall*). The fourth, *would,* is semantically parallel to *will* in an odd way: just as *will* has no meaning beyond laterness, so *would* has no meaning beyond lesser probability or lesser urgency; it often serves merely as a polite softener.

4.4.1. All of the modal auxiliaries are future-pointing, as compared with the primary constructions, of which twelve of the sixteen are past-pointing (those with Modifications I and II). The future-pointing is implicit in the semantic content of *can* (*could*), *may* (*might*), *dare, must, need, ought;* the exception is the occasional appearance of *could* as a true Past of *can*.

4.4.2. With *shall* (*should*), *will* (*would*) the future-pointing is explicit. *Shall* (except for its occurrence as "the correct future form" with "I/we") is used only in questions; it asks for instruc-

---

[7]When the construction Modal + *have* + past participle would be called for as "repetition" in the sense of 1.3.(4) above, the substitute formula is Modal + *have*: "Hadn't Don read your letter? He may have, but . . . .—I didn't think Doug would omit that item. Well, he shouldn't have, and he'll probably include it later.—He was strong enough to insist, and if he'd been wise he would have."

tion or suggestion about future behavior, as contrasted with "Will
. . .?" which asks for prediction. The unreal form *should* signals
a lesser degree of urgency in instruction or suggestion as to future
behavior; it occurs both without and with negation, in both questions and statements. *Will* explicitly and solely signals laterness.
It is specifically incompatible with the Past modification, but compatible with the other three primary modifications. ("He will
have traveled through seven countries by this time next week.
You'll be visiting the aunts, won't you? That will be revealed
in due time.") In its own inflection, *will* is incompatible with a
Past meaning. Hence *would* is its "Past" only in the functions of
sequence of tenses and unreality, not in the function of earlierness.
As we have seen, *would* signals unreality (lesser probability or urgency) per se without any further content, just as *will* signals futurity per se.

4.5. There are lacunae in the theoretically possible combinations of the modals with negative and interrogative constructions.
We find *can't, couldn't, shouldn't, won't, wouldn't* in both statements and questions. Regularly in statements but rarely in questions, we find *mustn't* and *needn't*. Following "not" is commoner
than "-n't" with *dare* and *might; may not* is far commoner than
mayn't, which is close to sounding like an affectation. *Shall not*
is rare, and *shan't* is almost archaic in statements. *Shall* itself is a
genteelism in affirmative statements, whether in the meaning of
futurity or as an instruction. *Oughtn't* is found in both questions
and statements, and *Ought* in questions, for many speakers; see below 5.4.3.

Adjuncts

5.0. The two sets of auxiliaries are closed lists, of fixed mem-
bership. The modals *dare, need, ought* are of limited combinability, comparatively infrequent, and may be entirely missing or
restricted to very few formulas in the grammar of some speakers
of English. Otherwise, the auxiliaries are stable sets.

5.1. The adjunct set is a relatively open list. It may be
entered from above, so to say, by decaying modals like *dare, need,
ought*, and from below by full verbs which attain formulaic status
in complex verb constructions ("get to see him, make him talk, have
a house built"). Except for the quasi-modal *ought* and the col-
loquial pseudo-modal "better," adjuncts share the formal features

of full verbs: they have the subject-agreement suffix -s; they require full "not" rather than "-n't"; most of them require the empty auxiliary *do* in negative, interrogative, and insistent constructions.

5.2. Simple adjuncts are "get" with -ing and with past participle, and "keep (on)" with -ing. Colloquially, "better" can function as a simple adjunct in statements, affirmative and negative; in questions it is preceded by *had*. Constructions like "begin, start, stop" + -ing are borderline items as simple adjuncts.

5.3. Complex adjuncts are marked by following "to": "have to, have got to (gotta), want to, used to, be able to, be about to, be supposed to, be to, be bound to, be going to." The complex adjuncts with *be* treat it as if it were a copula: i.e., -n't, no requirement of empty *do*. The modal auxiliaries *dare, need, ought* appear as adjuncts with "to." *Dare* and *need* appear with empty *do*. The usage of these three quasi-modals with "to" varies from speaker to speaker at present. Borderline adjuncts would include "try to, try and."

5.4.1. The grammatical status of adjuncts is their function as a repertory of available suppletions to fill in gaps in the auxiliary sets, to avoid grammatical ambiguities, to intensify or cancel the meaning of an auxiliary. Thus "had to" supplies a semantic Past for *must*. "Have to, have got to" are stylistic alternatives to *must*.[8] "Was/Were able to" performs a similar function for *can* and avoids the ambiguity of *could*: Past, or unreal?

5.4.2. "Get" + past participle may serve as an unmistakable passive, which avoids the ambiguity of "The door was closed": Passive; or copula + predicate adjective?[9]

5.4.3. "Ought to" fills the gap in the occurrence of *shall*, in statements; and "oughtn't to" fills the gap created by the lack of *shan't* in unaffected usage. (For some speakers, *ought* is a true modal auxiliary except in affirmative statements: "Ought we go? Oughtn't we go? We oughtn't go" but "We ought to go." For others, the form with "to" is used in statements and the true modal without "to" in questions. Yet others have "ought to" and *oughtn't* in both statement and question. With others, "ought to, oughtn't to" are regular in all usages.)

---

[8]"don't have to" is the semantic suppletion of "*must-not (go)" as distinct from "must'nt = must not-(go)."

[9]But note that another grammatical ambiguity may be involved: "get = become" + participle ("get thoroughly chilled").

5.4.4. The complex adjuncts with "be" convey various forms of laterness. "Be to = the special non-routine plan calls for"; "be supposed to = the routine schedule, design, etiquette, morality call for"; "be going to = a recent decision calls for"; "be about to = the event is imminent"; "be bound to = the event is certain."

5.4.5. "Keep (on)" + -ing cancels the later limit of a duration.

5.4.6. "Get" + -ing specifies the earlier limit of a duration.

5.4.7. "Used to" cancels current relevance, and is thus a denial of the meaning of *have been* + -ing (Modifications II and III): "I used to play tennis there. I have been playing tennis there."

5.5.1. All adjuncts are compatible with a following Modification III, *be* + -ing, except "keep (on), get" + -ing. All are compatible with a following Passive except "get" + past participle. The complex adjuncts with "be" and "ought, need to" can be followed by *have* + past participle (Modification II).

5.5.2. Most adjuncts can be preceded by modal auxiliaries and can themselves undergo the primary Modifications I (Past), II (Current relevance), and III (limited duration).

6.0. The combinability of the three sets is thus:

6.1. Adjuncts can precede any combination of the primary auxiliaries. There can be sequences of more than one adjunct: "I don't want to have to be able to keep + -ing."

6.2. Modals can precede any combination of the primary auxiliaries, and any of the adjuncts except "used to, be to, ought to." There cannot be more than one modal auxiliary in a construction.

6.3. The primary auxiliaries *have* and *be* can follow either a modal or an adjunct, and can immediately precede the full verb (with -ing or in the past participle form), and can precede an adjunct but not a modal.

6.4. The maximal order is thus: Modal auxiliary, primary auxiliaries, adjuncts, primary auxiliaries, lexical verb.

Part II

a sampling of courses and
programs in composition
and communication

chapter 6

THE COMMUNICATIONS PROGRAM AT BOSTON UNIVERSITY COLLEGE OF BASIC STUDIES *

Harry H. Crosby **

The freshman English program at Boston University College of Basic Studies can be understood — and appreciated — only if the curriculum of which it is part is known. The College is a two-year lower division program sixty-five per cent of whose approximately nine hundred students transfer to upper division work at Boston University or other colleges and universities. Its students take two years each of science, humanities (literature, music, art, and philosophy), social science, psychology and guidance, and communications. The program is aimed at liberal-general objectives, "liberal" in the sense that all the departments try to give historical, philosophical, psychological, and aesthetic perspectives to make critical judgments, and "general" in the sense that the program is non-vocational, but is aimed at broader problems of citizenship which require considerable reading and expression. Thus, the Communications Department enjoys a great deal of cooperation from the other departments in the development of critical thinking and effective communication habits.

Two other unique features, the team system of instruction and the Sophomore Utopian project, help the communication program. Our students are assigned in groups of approximately one hundred to a team of five instructors, one from each of the departments. These five instructors confer frequently to discuss the welfare of their students — in fact, they all share the same office

*Formerly Boston University Junior College.
**Chairman, Division of Communications.

— and the student ability which concerns all instructors in common is the ability to study and indicate possession of knowledge, *i.e.* reading, listening, writing, and speaking. Most of the instructors in the college require written work, and all of them use at least some essay tests. Thus, the communications teachers have unusual cooperation from other departments: it is not unusual at all, for instance, for a science teacher to help a student use phonics to improve his spelling or for a humanities teacher to help a student a great deal with diction or organization problems. With the instructional team all working together as a "college within a college," the training in communication can be all the more thorough since it comes from so many directions.

The Utopian project is a long paper prepared by Sophomore students in which they try to create an ideal society based upon their study of the previous two years. They try to show the contributions and role in the ideal society of the scientist, social scientist, artist and philosopher; they try to satisfy the social, physical, and psychic needs of its citizens. This project is supervised by the Humanities Department but here again the cooperation of the entire instructional team aids the communications instructor to teach research and writing techniques.

It may seem odd that so much of this program description has been devoted to the complete Basic Studies program but our curriculum is so tightly integrated that no part can be appreciated without an understanding of its entirety.

Within this context, the Communications Department has the primary objective of helping its students learn to communicate significant thoughts effectively. Since the students' first and most urgent need for these skills is in their study of other courses and their desire to be able to express what they have learned, the Communications staff is pleased to take advantage of this motivation and willingly assumes the role of a service department; whenever possible we key our assignments to the study and expression needs of the other departments. We use their lectures and reading assignments, for instance, to illustrate study techniques and problems of organization.

To achieve our objectives, the Communications staff knows no better method than to demand that our students read, write, listen, and speak frequently under close supervision. Each freshman is required, for example, to write a minimum of 16,000 words, that is, thirty-two 500 word themes per school year.

Correlative to this principle is the belief that students will be able to use the language better if they know a great deal about it. During the first semester, therefore, students study Hayakawa's *Language In Thought And Action*, and Dean and Wilson's *Essays On Language and Usage*. They are expected to pass tests on semantics, lexicography, language history and structure, dialect development, and usage. Recently our students have been asked, for instance, to write extemporaneous essay examination answers to these questions: (1) Discuss the differences between the language used by Americans in colonial times and today. (2) Briefly trace the development of the dictionary, citing at least five significant dictionaries and their contribution to lexicography. (3) Analyze the following nonsense sentence showing how its syntax can be determined by structure and position: *The cledums hypotheduzed eleatically.* (4) Show how linguists demonstrate the relationship between modern languages. Use these three sentences if necessary for illustration, and any other information you know. German: Ya, Mutter, ich habe drei; French: Oui, ma mère, jén ai trois,; and English: Yes, Mother, I have three. (5) Define *cognate, ladder of abstraction, euphemism, intonation, multiple negation, hyperbole, morpheme.*

As many as possible of the themes during the first semester are concerned with language problems. For instance, students are asked to analyze the referents of abstract language in texts, mass media, and advertising. They are asked to analyze the source of the scientific vocabulary they find in their text books. They are asked to contrast the dialects of Boston and New York students. They are asked to write themes about changes in language such as vowel shifts, metathesis, formation of acronyms, and adoption of loan words, changes that are occurring in their own tongue.

In order to supply our students with additional subject matter we have not found suitably presented in print, we have a weekly lecture series on such topics as the nature of communication, the history of the language, operational thinking, the history of style, and the intelligent use of mass media. The uniqueness of the lecture series, we think, lies in our attempt to bring these subjects into immediacy for the students. When students study language history, for example, they are given writing assignments which demonstrate that as in Anglo-Saxon times, there are examples of metathesis and vowel shift taking place today.

In spite of this rather heavy subject matter which students must master, we still think of ours as a skills program. We want our students to learn to study, to write, read, speak, and listen effectively. In the past, programs which started out as writing programs became literature programs or American Civilization programs when teachers became so fascinated with their content that they forgot about writing; it is so much more pleasant to talk about Melville than about commas. To avoid this we have the "theme-a-week" minimum requirement. More importantly, we organize our first semester by aspects of communication that we wish to teach. During the first three weeks, our students are reading Hayakawa, but while we are discussing the material, we constantly discuss study techniques. Using the text for practice material, students outline the chapters, demonstrate their use of the Survey-Question-Read-Recite-Review study technique, and prepare answers to essay-type examination questions. During the next units, students study the essays on language and usage but their classroom activity stresses, in order, purpose, organization, content, and style. We spend three weeks on each concept. Our students must learn the subject matter in the essays, but, during class discussion, instructors lead them through analysis of the way central ideas are advanced and made clear. They are shown how different purposes dictate different organizational patterns. They are shown how styles vary, how certain sentence patterns can be used effectively under certain circumstances, how figures of speech can be used for vividness and variety. Here again, we try to be extremely ambitious. Our students are supposed to understand such terms as *thesis, cause-to-effect organization, chronological development, transition, euphony, oxymoron,* and *hyperbole;* we hope their ability to communicate will improve as a result of their knowing the vocabulary and principles of composition.

During the second semester, our content shifts to material much more like the traditional program. We do use an anthology. We do not, however, downgrade the material. No student is ever allowed to think he is reading a collection of old magazine articles. Instead, we have selected a series of problems which we think are the important constantly recurring questions of general education. The anthology currently under preparation for our course takes up the problems of The World Around Me, The Search for Identity, Higher Education, Right and Wrong, Fact, Myth and Stereotype, and The Good Life. Our instructors try to emphasize throughout that these are problems which are terribly crucial to students and adults and that they are deep philosophical problems (The Nature of Man, Truth, and Good, etc.) and that there is great literature written about these problems.

During the analyses of these essays about these problems, instructors use them as models to buttress the previous training in purpose, organization, content, and style, with the emphasis being based either according to the nature of the essay or the problems of the students.

In summary, then, we try to give the students a thorough grounding in information about language during the first semester; in the second semester we introduce them to the great literature of basic questions of general education. In both semesters we are preoccupied with the techniques of good communication. In the second semester, our students again write their theme a week with the subject being their own attempts to find their own role in society, in combatting myth, deciding what is the education best suited for them, and so on as the content emphasis shifts from question to question.

One of the problems of organizing a freshman English program has been the staffing. Usually freshman English is taught by graduate students who are dutifully but often grimly putting in their apprentice period prior to their entering the lotus land of literature. The career freshman English instructor is rare indeed, in part because so little prestige and professional promise is attached to teaching the too often onerous subject. At Boston University we have quite frankly considered the instructor when the course was arranged; we wanted a course so filled with interesting and worthwhile material that it would be pleasurable to teach. We have been given unusual financial support in that our instructors have just as great an opportunity to climb up the professional ladder and attain as high salaries as in any other department. We consider our salary scale a favorable one, instructors $5,000-$5,600; assistant professors $5,600-$7,500; associate professors $7,500-$9,000, and full professors $9,000-$14,000. The loads, too, are favorable, we think. An instructor's four classes meet four times per week but one meeting is a general session for all sections; thus the instructor meets his classes thirteen hours per week.

A difficult aspect of the staffing problem is that English departments just do not turn out products who are prepared to teach Freshman English. Examine any Ph.D. transcript. You know that its possessor will undoubtedly have several survey courses in literature and many seminars in Shakespeare, Milton, Hawthorne, Melville, or whatever his area of concentration. He may have a course in the history of the English language, but he almost inevitably will have no academic preparation in rhetoric, linguistics, semantics, lexicography, dialect study, communication theory or logic — even though the subject matter of these courses will be the background of what he should teach his students. In recruiting the College of Basic Studies staff of Communications we tried to make the best of this bad situation. We deliberately selected candidates who had the most apprentice training in some of the best large Freshman English programs in the country: Indiana, Illinois, Wisconsin, Southern California, Iowa and Michigan— best in the sense that in addition to being sound programs in themselves, their administrators give thorough in-service training to graduate-assistant teachers. In addition we tried to find people who have academic training of most value. Members of our staff have studied rhetoric under Perrin, classical rhetoric at Columbia, semantics at Southern California, linguistics under Fries, Marckwardt, and Ives, and lexicography at Merriam-Webster. To get a wide distribution of viewpoints we have recruited teachers who have earned or are working on graduate degrees from Southern California, Washington, Stanford, Iowa, Illinois, Indiana, Michigan, Wisconsin, Brown, Harvard, Columbia, and Boston University — a group not without luster when it comes to assembling any kind of staff, let alone for Freshman English.

Another problem of staffing has given rise to the development of the internship program. We want to give our students full-time fully-trained instructors, but we still feel the responsibility of a university to give apprentice training to potential college teachers. In addition, we have a student-faculty ratio of 100 to one. an overload for a freshman English teacher. We therefore have awarded a three-fifths time appointment to Ph.D. candidates, one for each full-time instructor. Thus, each full-time instructor has a three-fifths time assistant who critiques half of the papers and assists during classroom activity, laboratories, and conferences. We have tried to work out an internship training that will give sound training for all teaching activity. In the course of his complete internship each graduate student will give several lectures to large groups of students, conduct many classes and laboratories, prepare many lesson plans, and make many judgments — all under the close supervision of a senior instructor. We are pleased to be able to pay the interns reasonably well: for twenty-five hours' work per week, he receives complete tuition for a year, including summers, and $1,800, totaling about $2,500. Each subsequent reappointment carries with it an increase of $200. A graduate load is made possible which means that the candidate should earn the Ph.D. in three years.

The communications program at Boston University is so new that it is difficult to write about the present; to write about the future is to deal in guesses. Nevertheless, the following changes and developments can be predicted with some assurance.

(1) Since the College is moving soon into new quarters, we are very conscious of surroundings. We have long been painfully aware that the elementary school teacher uses her classroom as a teaching aid: she surrounds herself with illustrations, charts, posters, and all kinds of teaching aids which, even if they do not aid instruction, do create a learning atmosphere. The college teacher, on the other hand, teaches in four bare walls. Our staff has become interested in the problem of how to use a building as a teaching device. We are using bulletin boards more extensively than ever before and we are developing exhibits to emphasize and illustrate certain principles. We are experimenting with new kinds of projectors. We are trying to give students more oral critiques by putting them on tape. A student can sit in a small room with paper in hand and tune in on a critique, thus saving the duplication of instructor's time once when he read it, and once when he finally got the student in to talk to him. We hope we will be able to design and utilize many effective innovations for our new building.

(2) We hope to upgrade the content of the course. For too long students in Freshman English have been reading old magazine articles and hearing for the thirteenth time the fact that an adverb is a word which modifies a verb, an adjective, or an-

other adverb.   We will continue with our efforts to give our students significant college-level material about linguistics, rhetoric, logic, and communication theory.   We will try to refine our second semester selections to the point where a student is conscious of meeting the great minds who are dealing with great ideas.   We are confident that this improvement will not be made at the expense of practice in the skills of writing, speaking, reading, and listening.

(3)   In our future staffing, we will support the efforts of those enlightened universities who realize that their English Ph.D. possessors teach something besides literature.   As programs develop instruction in language and composition, we will indicate our approval by hiring their graduates.

(4)   Our instructors differ from many college instructors in that we tend to teach but one course, and the preparation for it is a cooperative project.   This fact, plus the existence of a three-fifths time for every instructor means that our staff are not overworked hacks.   We hope that we will have creative energy left over to study our subject matter and the effectiveness of our course and thus constantly to improve it.   We are trying very hard to be evaluation-conscious; we hope that our improvements can be documented by controlled research technique.   Thus, as we come to know more about our language and how to teach its effective use, we will be making worthwhile contributions to knowledge and fulfill the research function of a university staff — we hope at no cost to the quality of our instruction.

chapter 7

ENGLISH 1A-B AT THE UNIVERSITY OF CALIFORNIA AT BERKELEY

*Josephine Miles**

For almost a century, English 1A-B at the University of California has been a course in reading English literature and writing about it. *Reading* has meant close consideration, in class, of three or four whole works per term, and further reading outside. *Writing* has meant weekly prose exposition, in or out of class, of the character of the literature and of ideas rising from it. *English literature* has meant British and American, avoiding problems of translation, and has meant work of a quality equal to that read in other courses in the department: in 1A, mostly expository prose; in 1B, narrative, satiric, lyric, and dramatic verse and prose.

Certain contexts of circumstance should be explained. First, all students entering the University must have a B average from high school, and must either pass a three-hour examination in "Subject A," in grammar and exposition, or take the remedial noncredit course at extra cost. Second, of the fifty percent who pass the examination and the rest who later pass the course, most, unless bound by special departmental requirements, may choose between English 1A-B and a comparable course given by the Department of Speech. In the College of Letters and Science all students must take one or the other. Only about half of the freshmen entering each year, therefore, are enrolled in English 1A-B. Third, the department's use of teaching assistants, graduate students preferably with Master's degrees, as apprentice teachers who attend class, read

*Chairman of English 1A-B, 1949-51, 1957-59.

three-fourths of the papers, confer with students, and take full responsibility for two or three weeks per term, enables each member of the department to teach at least one section, thirty students, without being overburdened. Assuming these conditions, the following statements of procedure for those interested in teaching the course have been worked out by Professor John E. Jordan and the staff.

English 1A

PURPOSE: English 1A is a basic course for the English major and for the University. The aims of the course are two: (a) to teach students to write good expository prose, and (b) to teach them to read good expository prose. Although these aims can be reached only if we also teach students to think, the course is not expected to become primarily a course in formal logic. It is fundamentally a course in exposition, and the emphasis remains on writing and reading, on rhetorical pattern in the development of ideas in sentence, paragraph, and whole text.

PROCEDURES: *Class* — Class hours are normally devoted to some combination of the following four procedures: (a) discussion of principles of composition, perhaps in conjunction with assigned readings in a handbook; (b) discussion and analysis of assigned readings from expository texts; (c) discussion and analysis of student prose; (d) class exercises. Profitable work with student prose is possible by the use of mimeographed themes or the opaque projector with which the principal classroom is equipped. Little class time is devoted to formal instruction in grammar, because in order to take 1A and 1B a student must have passed either the examination or the course in Subject A.

Conference — Much of the best teaching is done in individual conferences. Students are required to confer with the instructor or the teaching assistant regularly. Some such device as not recording grades until the conference may be adopted to insure compliance. Students are usually asked to bring in a revised paper, and often required to present their accumulated corrected essays. Conferences may also be used for helping a student to define a subject before writing or for discussing special individual assignments of a more or less remedial character. Grammatical problems are usually handled in conference.

Writing — Students are required to write from 8,000 to 10,000 words of expository prose. This total includes occasional class exercises and essays written outside of class, which are usually assigned weekly. The normal practice is to begin with short essays and proceed to longer papers, one of which may be a paper requiring library "research" and introducing the students to elementary documentation. These essays must be corrected by the end of the semester and kept on file in the instructor's office for six months.

Standards — An adequately limited and focused idea and sound structure are considered essential. A paper which does not have a point is an F paper. Emphasis is placed on the ability to make a useful generalization and develop it coherently.

Student prose is expected to deal responsibly with ideas. For this reason, essay assignments often most effectively involve reading or other material which can be checked for accuracy of observation and emphasis.

Student prose is required to be correct in diction, idiom, grammar, punctuation, and technical form.

Marking — Essays are marked promptly and returned as soon as possible. Technical and rhetorical errors are marked on the papers, often by a system of symbols explained in the assigned handbook. A specific comment is added to each paper as an explantion of the grade. The comments are, if possible, encouraging; they are definite and constructive. They often require that the paper be written or revised, in part or in full. They are initialed by the reader and include instructions to confer if a conference on the assignment is required.

Reading: *Rationale* — The purposes of reading expository texts are generally these: (a) to show students how practiced writers deal with compositional problems, (b) to prepare students to read effectively the expository prose of their college texts and other serious work, and (c) to provide common bodies of ideas for class discussion in problems of organization and responsible treatment and for use in essay assignments. The expository texts may assist in giving a thematic unity to the course, provided that unit is one appropriate to an English course in expository writing.

Students are held responsible for the content of the readings — otherwise we could hardly teach good habits of reading — but care is taken not to allow the subject matter of the readings to become the primary subject of the course. In studying the expository texts, primary emphasis is put on the way in which meaning has been embodied in form.

Texts — Texts are selected by individual instructors. The staff requirements are that each instructor assign a good dictionary, a handbook of grammar, and two or three volumes of expository prose, of which *at least* one is a full-length book of expository prose by one author. The staff list is illustrative of the kind of books used, expository prose of the 19th and 20th centuries, of quality comparable with that of the literature read in other courses in the department. Members of the staff disagree about the usefulness of many of these, but agree on listing them as possibilities. For example: *Education of Henry Adams,* Arnold's *Culture and Anarchy,* Becker's *Freedom and Responsibility,* Eliot's *Notes toward a Definition of Culture,* Emerson's *Essays,* Mill on *Liberty,* Orwell's *Essays,* Russell's *Authority and the Individual,* Shaw's *Prefaces,* Thoreau's *Walden.*

English 1B

PURPOSE: English 1B is the sequel to 1A, which is prerequisite to it. It aims to maintain the skills in reading and writing achieved in 1A and to develop the skills of reading imaginative literature. Its emphasis is on close and careful reading of a few literary texts. Its discipline is accuracy, full savoring rather than wide skimming.

PROCEDURES: *Class* — Class time is spent chiefly in close analysis of the texts and general class discussion of the meaning, the devices for expressing that meaning, and the literary effects achieved. The discussions are usually on a rather elementary level: The students ordinarily have difficulties in simply understanding the texts so that there is little opportunity for more sophisticated critical analysis — which is the province of English 100. The instructor needs to provide a certain amount of background in literary and social history and may exploit a chronological arrangement of the texts, but he keeps the emphasis on the individual texts, not the history — which is the province of English 46A-B.

Frequent short quizzes to check on the accuracy of the students' reading are routine. These quizzes include paraphrases, questions of fact, and questions of interpretation. There are at least two class essays or midterms and a stiff final examination. The examination usually tests the students' ability to paraphrase and comment upon passages of Elizabethan English which they have not previously read, to identify significantly passages from assigned texts, and to write essays making thematic connections between their readings.

Conferences   Individual conferences with instructors and teaching assistants are held as in 1A. They have the same function of meeting the student's special problems and talking about his writing. Writing: Students are required to write, as in 1A, from 8,000 to 10,000 words of expository prose. A larger percentage of this total than in 1A, however, is usually taken up in class writing and in longer papers. It is generally advisable to begin early in the semester with short essays and to require perhaps four papers of 1,000 to 1,500 words.

Standards — The standards of expository prose are those applied in 1A. In addition, 1B papers are expected to show some literary awareness. Thus an A paper is one which is excellent in critical perceptiveness, in logical coherence, and in grammatical and technical correctness; a B paper good, a C paper adequate, a D paper below average, and an F paper failing in these respects.

Reading: Instructors select editions of the texts and teach them in any order that they wish. Instructors may assign supplementary readings; however, the department has voted that since 1B is intended as a single course with a common core of readings in all sections, supplementary readings should be used only as they facilitate the study of the central texts and should not be allowed to usurp the class time for close analysis of the central readings.

The required reading in the course is Shakespeare, narrative and satiric prose, and poetry, specifically for one year as follows: *Hamlet, Henry IV Part I, Gulliver's Travels, The Major Poets,* (Ed., Coffin).

#

The course has been stable for so long that I doubt there will be any great change by 1970. In my memory of the 1940s and 1950s, the present center was strongly held. The differences of opinion, bases for hours of biweekly staff deliberation, are themselves fairly constant. There is usually one minority more interested in ideas and states of mind than in details of texts; there is usually another group especially interested in a direct and detailed study of the language as literary medium, semantically or linguistically. But the strength of the texts and of the students' need for formulating understanding of them provides a center about which agreement is not difficult. Agreement is that the English literary tradition, rational and imaginative, provides the best impetus for the development of the students' own reason and imagination in reading and writing.

chapter 8

ENGLISH COMPOSITION AT CARNEGIE INSTITUTE OF TECHNOLOGY

*Neal Woodruff, Jr.**

English Composition, C-703 and C-704, is given to a diverse group of professional students at Carnegie Institute of Technology, among them engineers, chemists, physicists, biologists, students of industrial management and printing management, home economists, students of secretarial and business methods, and students of education. The group includes all freshmen at Carnegie except those in the College of Fine Arts, who take another course that has somewhat broader subject matter. C-703 and C-704 are three-hour courses which meet for the customary three periods per week. They are taught in sections of about 25 which are as heterogeneous professionally as scheduling permits them to be.

The course has one controlling aim: to prepare students to write maturely and effectively in both their professional and their non-professional lives after college. There are several exclusions implied by this aim. First, students are not taught to write as college students for professors. We are, of course, concerned that they write as well as they can and that they gain in maturity while they are in college. We intend that they shall learn to explore and present ideas, to convey their knowledge lucidly in papers and examinations, and to set forth the results of research. But we do not give the course an academic emphasis, nor do we devote any great proportion of our teaching time explicitly to the problems of writing in college courses. Second, students are not taught

*Associate Professor of English.

"self-expression." We assume that good writing is not just a matter of getting something successfully off one's chest, but of successfully adapting what one says to the situation which calls it forth. This involves meeting demands imposed upon the writer from outside, and meeting them in a deliberate, controlled way. Herein lies the discipline of writing, as we conceive it, not merely in finding words that express one's mind. Finally, students are not trained in specialized writing techniques such as those of technical or business writing. There is no predicting what sorts of situations they will later have to deal with in writing. If writing is to be a means of adaptation, it must be taught as an adaptable skill, in a way that looks toward variety in the demands made upon the writer.

In terms of pedagogy, then, the basic aim of the course is to teach fundamental knowledge and fundamental skills. Teaching is directed primarily toward future learning and secondarily toward immediate improvement in ability to write. If the student can be equipped with knowledge and skills which are widely applicable to writing situations, if he can be taught what in general he must take account of in such situations, he can refine and augment what he knows as he applies it in particular instances, academic and non-academic. We teach the course on the assumption and in the hope that the student will later become a better writer than we are able to make him during his freshman year. Our aim is to begin a process of sophistication.

The course gains its orientation toward fundamentals from an emphasis placed throughout on communication. This does not mean, it must be made clear, that it is a course broadly concerned with "communication skills." It includes no training in speech or reading, no concern with the arts or the mass media (except incidentally, as something read touches upon these things), and no emphasis upon criticism. It is as purely a course in expository writing as we can make it. The concept of communication is crucial because it provides the standards by which writing is judged. At the beginning of the course, students are introduced to the view that the purpose of writing is to convey something out of one mind into another and that such a purpose imposes obligations upon the writer. As the course progresses, the nature of those obligations unfolds. Organization, for example, is taught as a means of arranging what one has to say in the way that makes it most readily available to the audience intended.   Punctuation is taught partly as a means of achieving clarity of statement and partly as a matter of conventions which one observes out of consideration for readers. Economy and directness of statement are taught as ways of avoiding needless labor for readers, which is also a matter of consideration. Care in managing connotations is taught as a means of achieving an appropriate tone, of establishing the relationship one wishes to establish with the reader.   Everywhere the question considered is how to make written communication effective.

This emphasis on communication is present for two chief reasons, one concerning the teaching of writing as a discipline, the other concerning the teaching of it as an adaptable skill.   If writing is to be a discipline, there must be standards to be met.   Further, those standards must be in some way objective and meaningful, not simply arbitrary.   Most students have learned, by the time they reach college, that many of the prescriptions made in grammar books have for them high nuisance value and no very great utility. They need to learn that standards for writing can be functional, that paragraphing is more than a schoolmarm's whim and punctuation more than a pedagogue's obsession.   An emphasis on communication allows such things to be justified precisely by their utility. It allows the student to find writing a meaningful activity regulated by standards for which he can see some reason.   He comes to understand that the need for precision, clarity, and economy in writing is constant, and that certain primary methods of producing them are constant as well.

There are other aspects of writing which are not constant, and an emphasis on communication also takes account of those. We are convinced that the great lack in much writing, especially writing done by specialists, is the failure of writers to recognize that they create human relationships.   Everyone who writes presumably writes to be read, and yet the ability to acknowledge the fact in the way one writes is, except among professional writers. quite rare.   The specialist often seems to write in a vacuum, wrestling only with his specialty and not acknowledging an obligation to make it fully available, perhaps to someone with very definite interests or requirements.   As we make use of the idea, communication implies not only the general obligation to be precise, clear, and economical, but the specific obligation to direct what one writes to the audience one intends. Audiences vary greatly: they are broad or narrow; they are differently educated or informed; they sometimes want to put what they read to some special use which is known to the writer; they must be approached with different sorts of tact. The skillful writer, we think, takes account of the nature of his audience and of the situation in which he writes. He allows these things to determine his choice of words, his way of writing sentences, even his way of organizing what he has to say. The student who is to become skillful must learn to take account of these things and must begin to make some judicious choices.

So much for the aims and the dominant emphasis of the course. They are implemented by a number of teaching techniques which have evolved through the cooperative work of the staff over the past thirteen years. These techniques, insofar as they are special, concern three aspects of teaching the course: formulating writing assignments, using various sorts of reading material as subject matter for writing, and instructing in the classroom.

Students in the course are required to write about one theme a week during the year, a total approaching thirty. Slightly more than half are carefully prepared outside of class; the remainder are written during a fifty-minute class period, usually on a subject announced at the beginning of the period. With the possible exception of the first two or three themes written in the course, none are "open-ended" assignments which call for an account of personal experience or the expression of personal reaction. These things may be involved as elements of a theme, but from almost the beginning of the course, assignments specify not only a subject or question but also a reader and situation and purpose. These latter are specified in varying degrees, and the course moves on the whole from simple and general sorts of communication to the more complex and specific.

The nature of the assignments can be illustrated by two typical examples, both based on *Huckleberry Finn*. The first is:

> Explain for someone who has not read *Huckleberry Finn* what views Huck holds on conventional religion.

The assignment asks simply for an account of some facts which the student has at his disposal. But in setting them forth he has to remember that his reader is unacquainted with their context. He has to give background. He must briefly introduce Huck and place him in his setting. He must suggest the experience which accounts for Huck's opinion. He must make matters clear to a reader whose knowledge is slighter than his own. The second assignment is:

> For the fellow-members of your class, write a convincing answer to this question: How intelligent and resourceful is Huckleberry Finn?

The question involves some students at first in a problem of coming to terms with the novel. Their initial impulse, born of their confusion of intelligence with education, is to think Huck's lack of refinement a sign of his lack of intelligence. The assignment compels them to gather evidence which soon convinces most of them that despite his unvarnished manner, Huck is indeed both intelligent and resourceful. But, having entertained the other opinion, they are aware of the need to muster evidence for an airtight case. They see the possibility that their audience will have to be convinced of their judgment of the facts, and consequently they endeavor not only to establish their view but to controvert the view that they have rejected.

Both of these examples are from the first semester of the course. Two others from the second semester will show how the assignments become more difficult. One is based on the students' study of connotation. This subject is introduced near the beginning of the semester because students will go on to consider how tone is established and will be confronted with assignments requiring them to achieve tact. After connotation has been discussed and exemplified during two or three class periods, this writing assignment is sometimes given:

> Write an explanation, to be read by a high school freshman of 14 or so, of what connotations are.

The audience here is more narrowly specified, and a particular purpose is plainly implied — to make the explanation clear to someone who has not encountered the term before and who is unlikely to have thought much about semantic properties of words. A little thought will reveal to the student that a highly abstract definition will not do, even though he now understands that definition himself. It will reveal, too, that examples can neither be thrown in indiscriminately nor left unapplied to the idea being explained. If he is ingenious, the student may think of slang terms familiar to the high school freshman which will illustrate his point.   In any case, he must adapt his explanation to the knowledge and capacity to understand of the 14-year-old, as he can best estimate those things.   The other advanced assignment is one we have sometimes given near the end of the second semester when students have completed the reading of Robert Penn Warren's

All the King's Men:

> A member of your family has written you, after hearing that *All the King's Men* is read in your English course, to say that he disapproves of your being required to read it.   He thinks it a demoralizing book, full of profanity and smutty language, and containing indecent passages. If you disagree with his judgment, write for him a defense of your being asked to read the book.   If you agree, write an essay expressing your view, which is to be read by the committee of teachers who will choose books for next year's course.

This assignment is deliberately tough.   The student's problem is not only to make his case, to present his judgment and substantiate it convincingly, but to do so in a way that does not offend a reader whose judgment he finds wrong.   Because there are so many imponderables when someone is emotionally involved in a question, there is no such thing as a perfectly correct response to the assignment.   But the student must show by the way he writes that he takes full account of the need for tact.

It should be plain that assignments of this sort enforce our emphasis on communication.   The student learns through doing them that before all else he must consider reader and situation, that even before he plans what he wants to say he must analyze these things and allow his conclusions to shape his plan.   In order to focus sharply the importance of these considerations, we have sometimes made use of dual problems, in which the same subject matter is to be conveyed to two different audiences.   If, from such assignments, the student learns to try always to put himself in his reader's shoes, he will have learned the lesson that will later, we think, prove of greatest value to him as a writer.

As subject matter for most writing assignments, we use reading materials, both exposition and fiction.   In large part, we use them to provide rather directly the subjects for writing assignments as the source of ideas or situations upon which the student writes commentaries of a specified sort. When he is reading exposition, the student may be asked to digest an essay for a reader who has a special use for an epitome. Or he may be asked to express, for someone of opposing view, his agreement or disagreement with a position taken in an essay. Occasionally he may be asked to apply ideas encountered in an essay to an actual or hypothetical situation in his own life. As the basis for such assignments, we try to find exposition which communicates fully and immediately to the student. We hope it will capture his interest, but we try to be sure at least that it is writing which his background enables him to comprehend readily. Except when a writing assignment is designed to result from research, we prefer that the student be able to concentrate on writing and that he not be diverted by an effort to understand what he finds difficult or obscure.

The use made of fiction in the course has some special characteristics. We find that as subject matter fiction has the advantage of being concrete rather than abstract, of being something which resembles real experience. Exposition and fiction, that is, differ in the way they function as subject matter: assignments based on exposition give the student practice in managing and applying ideas which have been supplied to him; those based on fiction require him to discover and structure ideas for himself. Because the course is concerned almost exclusively with writing, we do not teach fiction as literature. Essentially, we use it as case material. We choose novels not so much for their literary merit as for the fact that they are readily understandable (which means, usually, that they are realistic in technique) and that their major concerns are set forth rather obviously as themes. We have used with some success, for example, *Huckleberry Finn, All the King's Men, The Rise of Silas Lapham, The Late George Apley, The Moon and Sixpence,* and *Of Human Bondage.* We do not treat them as the products of creative minds, or of times and places, or of literary styles and movements. Rather, we enter into an unspoken conspiracy with the students to regard events and characters as actual, and ask them, in their themes, to write about the significance of those events and characters.

Classroom instruction in the course is designed to enable students to learn from the writing assignments based on these readings. For the most part, instruction is carried on by discussion. We speak of it as "inductive" teaching, though much of it involves no formal inductive process. The essential thing is that classroom work is dominantly discussion of the writing assignments given and the papers written in response to them. It is necessary, especially early in the course, to discuss with students the demands made by the assignments they are given. They are not used to writing in response to assignments which specify reader and situation, and at first they are uncertain how they are expected to take these things into account. It would be easy, of course, to give explicit directions. But because the purpose of instruction is to enable them later to analyze writing situations individually and unaided, it seems well from the very start to give them practice by means of directed group discussion. Sometimes, too, such preparatory discussion is concerned with analyzing not the writing situation but the subject matter to be dealt with. Students are given practice in perceiving clearly what their subject is, and in choosing and applying relevant evidence. Preparatory discussion of these kinds occurs at various times in the course when new complications are introduced in writing assignments or when subject matter presents new difficulties.

The bulk of class discussion, however, arises from the writing the students have done. We make a practice of giving uniform assignments to a class. The advantage gained is that each student, having completed the same assignment as the others, is well qualified to judge the results and usually eager to discuss them. Much of the most fruitful classroom work in the course arises out of a class's interest in pooling experience. They are, we find, very hard on the shortcomings of their peers' work and very quick to praise what they find worthy. Their judgments, once they receive a little guidance, are surprisingly sound and perceptive. A good deal of our instruction in standards of effectiveness in communication is done through presenting a class with work written by its members and reproduced in some form, and simply asking for comments. The teacher channels discussion by choosing examples which exhibit virtues or faults that he wants the class to notice and by participating, without too pontifical a stance, in the discussion. Here, too, we do the major part of our teaching of grammar and mechanics. The teacher may present, at a time he finds appropriate, several examples of the same lapse in student writing. Or, he may simply digress from a single example to given general instruction on a point.

Teaching of this kind, dependent as it is on students' perceptions, may seem likely to become aimless. If the teacher is skillful, it does not in fact become so. A good deal depends upon his selection of examples and his guidance of discussion. But he must also frequently draw the class's attention away from the particulars on which its attention is focussed and demand that it formulate general conclusions. If his teaching is effective, his students gain not only experience in dealing with particular subjects and situations, but general principles to guide them as they continue to deal with these things.

Such, then, are the aims and methods of English Composition at Carnegie. The course is well established as it is given, and it seems unlikely that it will change greatly in the near future. Its aims are integrated with those of the whole program in professional education which Carnegie offers, and consequently they are firmly established. Its methods have changed somewhat, but gradually, as teachers' experience has modified them. In recent years some use has been made by individual teachers of concepts drawn from structural grammar, and it seems likely that those which prove most fruitful will come to be more widely used among us. There is perpetual discussion among members of the staff about the way reading matter can be best used and the way writing assignments can be best formulated. The staff includes teachers who find fiction more useful to them than exposition and others who find the reverse. It includes some who prefer to leave the writing situation general in making assignments and others who prefer to make it very specific. We have found place for all these preferences in the course. At present, with the aims and methods of the course generally but, we think, clearly defined, as much latitude as possible is left to the individual teacher.

chapter 9

THE COMMUNICATION PROGRAM AT DIABLO VALLEY COLLEGE

*Richard Worthen**

Diablo Valley College, a public junior college, accepted its first students in 1950. The college population has burgeoned in ten years from 294 to 1935 full time students, and the English staff has increased proportionately. Such growth inevitably presents a staff with both problems and opportunities: Problems because agreements and practices worked through at one time must be re-examined and evaluated with new staff members if there is to be *a* freshman English course offered, a course with a common conceptual center. Opportunities because new staff members bring strengths and insights which challenge any tendencies of the course of study to become encrusted and monolithic.

For the English staff at DVC all this has made for an interesting way of life and for a mode of operation which the administration has encouraged and supported. The English staff meets at least once a week for one hour, this meeting being a part of the instructor's regularly scheduled time. There is assessment by the staff of classroom practices, course content and philosophy. It would be merely wishful to report that staff meetings are regular periods of reasonable and frank discussion. They are not always. They draw near to or recede from that ideal as the instructor's subject matter awareness grows, as philosophical commitments crys-

---

*Instructor in English. This statement was prepared with the help and criticism of Karl O. Drexel, Director; George Madison, Dean of Instruction; and Wendell Johnson, Robert Martincich, Willis Middleton, William Sparke, William Miller, Communication staff members.

talize or dissolve and as unarticulated feelings emerge. The result is sometimes unsettling to those who crave peace and would accept superficial or showcase agreements. That our meeting time with its periodic irrelevancies and seeming lack of direction *is* nevertheless well spent is a truth that becomes apparent to some staff members only after they have experienced this way of life. But in time it becomes clear that the game is worth the candle. The courses remain alive; the staff faces its own communication obligations. It learns that surface tranquility with overt but simmering politeness can be too costly in some situations. There is a communication lesson for the staff in its own conduct.

The basic freshman English course is called Communication 120-121, Skills of Communication. It is that course whose shape has grown out of the commitments of DVC as a public junior college, out of a faculty-debated educational philosophy and out of the beliefs, knowledge and professional integrity of the English staff.

The underlying rationale for the communication course is related to the observation that the college freshman — who has usually thought very little about what goes on when men communicate in various modes and with various media — can find a meaningful and revealing subject matter in exploring the phenomenon of men communicating. To ask what goes on when men communicate is to give the student at least a first impression of breaking with much of his past experience in English classes. Depending upon his past success as a student of English and his willingness to take a new look at what is partly an old thing, the student qualifies his enthusiasm, but he seldom views the new subject with indifference. That he cannot honestly label the course "more of the same old thing" is no doubt a value to strive for; nevertheless the staff does not seek novelty except as it reflects concepts that they have explored and adopted as sound.

The student puzzles over and wrestles with a handful of terms that are new to him: *symbol, structure, gestalt, perception, culture, reality*. During his one or two semesters in communication he uses these terms with increasing comfort and understanding, finding that one aspect of the course consists in working out more and more solid understandings of them. *Structure* is a key concept in Communication 120-121; and something which gives it focus and rigor is the following: "Men communicate by using agreed-upon symbols to evoke more or less similar structures of meaning and feeling in each other's minds." What exactly *Mind* and *to evoke* mean we do not pretend to "know," of course. These and other key terms suggest the best constructs we know. The student finds them no more difficult than were some other, more shopworn, constructs that have been used in his earlier experience to hold the pieces of "English" together. We try to face the fact that the modern world is giving us more complicated pieces to hold together and that more comprehensive constructs are called for.

If the staff does not give the unanimous stamp of approval to each detail of the above description of the communication act, they do maintain the focus on communication, pressing the student — as receiver — to describe *how* this sentence, paragraph, essay, poem or film communicates; and conversely *how* he — as communicator — must make his own thoughtfully considered focusing idea emerge from patterned detail for his reader, how he must visualize his reader, estimate accurately his reader's role and background and then choose language appropriate to these. There is general agreement on the staff that the learner ultimately settles with himself *what* he knows when he has to present it stopped and crystalized in written symbols, that the quality of the knowing is reflected in the quality of the expression. This premise of learning we agree calls for a great deal of writing. As the student grows in his understanding of the concepts of the course he learns that their meaning has always been a part of his experience. This growth of understanding comes from experiencing, from reading, writing, observing, thinking and analyzing with a new consciousness of the nature and demands of these activities.

It would be misleading, however, to give undue emphasis to what some will no doubt be quick to label bizarre features of the course, features that are highlighted by the terms *symbol, structure, gestalt,* etc. If the course is symbol centered, it is, furthermore, *verbal* symbol centered. As with most freshman English courses, ours calls upon students to write and read far more than most have done in their previous schooling. They experience the normal freshman trauma in facing up to the demands of a course that calls for large amounts of carefully planned and executed writing, for careful reading of what seems to some a shocking amount of difficult material and for analysis of written material, theirs and other's, which demands that they perceive in detail the structure of that which communicates.

The following statement adopted by the staff in the last accreditation study of Diablo Valley College, more fully outlines our objectives and aims, and the topics studied:

Course Outline for Communication 120-121

I. *Statement of the Objectives of the Course:*

The objectives of this course are to help the student acquire knowledge and understanding:

A. Of how communication, especially language, functions as the matrix of human experience

B. Of the principles of logical thinking and of how they relate to expression and interpretation

C. Of the uses and abuses of persuasive appeals

D. Of the methods of effective organization of ideas and materials for expression and interpretation

E. Of similarities and differences of written and spoken English

F. Of standards of American English, especially those our students must meet at the junior college and in later life

G. Of standards and techniques of acceptable speaking in those situations our students will be in

H. Of how to locate and use reference and source materials

I. Of literature as a source of vicarious experience and of insights for understanding self and the world around us

J. Of the importance of close reading to develop the student's awareness of the author's intent

K. Of the idea that two-way communication promotes personal growth, whereas one-way communication is incipiently authoritarian, discouraging personal involvement and growth

II. *Topical Outline:*

Communication 120 — The more specific aims of this course are to help the student assess his feelings about "English"; to develop a consciousness of the communication concept and its application to the major affairs of his life, in society generally and more particularly in his academic efforts; and to develop skills in communication.

A. Orientation

1. Examining the place of communication in the general curriculum

2. Encouraging the student to examine his attitude toward English

    3. Developing the concept that men communicate by using agreed-upon symbols to evoke similar structures of meaning and feeling

B. Organization

    1. Learning to organize material through recognizing that reading, writing, listening, speaking, observing and critical thinking are directed toward communicating a structure of ideas which support a thesis

    2. Learning to create and present in a workmanlike manner structures of meaning and feeling.

C. The Nature of Language — Using the descriptive approach to language, to clarify levels of usage, the differences between written and spoken English, and the processes of growth and change in language

    1. Speech is the living language and sensitive, critical listening is the major resource for improving speech

    2. The written language only roughly approximates speech, and wide critical reading is the major resource for improving writing

Communication 121 — The more specific aim of this course is to give the student ample practice in reading, writing, listening, speaking and critical thinking. Particular emphasis is placed on close reading to develop the student's awareness of author's intent.

A. Critical Thinking — A systematic study of structure in the relationship between language and critical thinking

B. Poetry and the Short Story — A study of structure in the relationship between language and feeling

C. The Mass Media — A study of the potential of the mass media and the relationships between critical thinking and the devices, content, and effects of the mass media

D. The Film — Studied intensively as a typical medium of mass communication

    1. The one-wayness of the film

    2. The tendency towards over-simplification

    3. The impact of pictures

    4. The non-discursive elements reinforcing the message

E. Group Discussion — Introduction to the techniques and theory of group discussion and its importance in democratic society

F. The Term Paper — the object of this study is to give the student experience in organizing his thinking on a fairly abstract concept, such as maturity, the artist, the culture, the scientific approach to life, etc., which he has investigated through reference and source material and through the reading of novels which explore some aspect of the concept

Within the unifying framework of communication, the student finds coherence in such diverse reading selections as those of Dewey on the symbol, Sapir on the social functions of language, Leedy and Adler on the importance and complexity of reading, Seldes on the banalities, threats and potentialities of the mass media, Roberts on the structure of English, Daiches, Ciardi and others on the intent, value and structure of literature — and, of course, he reads and discusses literature.

This course itself and the previously mentioned way of life of our staff have been our major attempts at experimentation, and while the abilities of graduates of our course as we have observed them have corroborated the values of the course, we are at present conducting a testing program which we hope will give us some more objective evidence of our relative success or failure. In addition, we have always exchanged informally instructional material and methods, some of which might be labelled experimental. Perhaps the most notable characteristic of our experimental endeavours has been the range of attempts to help the student understand structure. Here are a few examples:

The student is given sentences which are linguistic blanks into which he inserts his own lexical meanings so that he is able to see just what he is doing when he "creates" a symbolic structure which communicates clearly. These arbitrarily structured sentences often result in awkward and "un-English" expression which calls for revision and which gives focus and concreteness to problems of diction.

The student is given scrambled paragraphs, i.e. sentences which lend themselves to a clearly best order. In reordering these he sees that a well chosen paragraph reveals a principle of rhetoric, that structure occurs in hierarchies, i.e. certain sentences fall into groups which are in turn so related as to create the one best whole.

The student is given an uncompleted outline of a speech on tape or of an expository movie and asked to complete the outline of the total structure after careful listening or viewing with note-taking.

The student expands a sentence into a paragraph or an article but does not use the sentence itself as a part of the paragraph or article. He creates a structure of ideas that forces the larger unifying idea upon the attention of the reader.

The student studies a fragmented film. He reads the script, then hears the sound track, then sees the film without sound; and finally he sees the whole. A tightly integrated, symbolically powerful film such as *Picture in Your Mind* is not intelligible until the total structure is presented.

#

We are definitely not satisfied that our present experiments should result in a static program. Since continued growth and our mode of operation make experiment, at least on an informal basis, inevitable, we shall try to improve our course insofar as we are capable. Improvement in the near future may include the following:

1. *Find ways to help the student work at his best pace.* This would involve carefully prepared supplementary units or "packages" of activities that the student would carry out through consultation with the instructor, through the listening to, reading and viewing of material supplementary to the normal classroom experience, but not independent of it and certainly not in place of it. This supplementary work should provide a way for the student to do *more* work, work that is more rigorously meaningful to him. It would point up for him *his needs* through repeated listening, reading and viewing experiences and expand and enrich his total communication experience to the degree that he assimilated it. Communication explorations could be conducted and assignments of a problem solving nature could be posed. Such activities would seek to offer the student the chance to teach himself convincingly the limits and the range of his capacities and they would expand for him the meaning of freedom to learn. Such a program would be expensive and should not by any means be thought of as an economy measure. It would call for equipment, for released time for instructors to plan and prepare, and for added secretarial help; and it would, I think, involve no less classroom time with smaller groups. Its *raison d'etre* should be to expand and deepen learning, not to save dollars.

2. *Finding ways to support the humanistic values.* This would call for our abandoning the currently fashionable dichotomy between the elite and the popular arts and

for giving the film and other media a new prominence. A study of *how* the work of art communicates can be made partly through such "laboratory" assignments as discussed above and without great expenditure of class-room time. The film room, the library and the listening booth can make available to the student leisurely and repeated reading, listening and viewing for analysis of the form and content of poetry, music, drama and painting. Increased literacy in the picture and in sound will not only enrich the student's aesthetic capacities but train him to cope with the products of the electronic tube. The good film in one sense combines the efforts of the poet, plastic artist and musician. Of course, such a program would not consist of casual reading, viewing and listening. There are exciting analogies to be developed between the forms of the poem, of music, of the novel and of the film. These can be studied to reveal the common elements in the symbolic experience. We need such understandings to help us maintain that minimum of unity and coherence in our symbolic life that allows us to deal with contemporary problems of freedom and to intelligently demand freedom. Within the limits of their understanding free men strive to use symbols for their beneficent effects; they try to avoid being used by symbols.

chapter **10**

THE FRESHMAN COURSE AT GENERAL MOTORS INSTITUTE

Robert E. Tuttle*

1. *The present course: its rationale, materials and methods.*

   a. *Context*

   At General Motors Institute, the Freshman English course has drawn its particular character from the context in which it is offered — the school and the sequence of related courses.

   General Motors Institute is a cooperative engineering college. During the first four years, at four or eight week intervals, the student alternates work at a General Motors plant with study in residence at the school. The total "year" includes forty-eight weeks. During a fifth year at the plant, the student completes an engineering project directly related to his field of work, the project culminating in a report. Upon satisfactory completion, he receives a bachelor's degree in Mechanical or Industrial Engineering.

   The students are a relatively homogeneous group with generally well defined personal objectives. They have high interest in things, especially mechanical ones. Admission is selective, so that, with rare exceptions, high school preparation is strong.

   During each work period each student writes a "coordination report," ranging from ten typed pages upwards, which is read and graded by his immediate supervisor and at least one other member of his plant's management. It is also

*Chairman, Department of English.

graded by the English Department. Most plant personnel have established high expectations of accuracy, clearness and appearance for these reports, and let the student know it. As a result, the English teacher rarely has any problem in motivating the beginning student, who perceives English as an important tool of professional communication. The student has much less interest in English as the stuff of communication for ideas outside his field, or as literature. As an upperclassman, however, he welcomes thinking and writing about ideas, and reading literature — he seems to reach a point in his maturation where he feels a real need and readiness to expand his intellectual and emotional world beyond the technical.

In view of this situation, the Freshman English course at the Institute has been established as just the beginning of a sequence of courses required in the area. The total sequence has the following required subjects (social studies and humanities other than English are excluded from this list):

English Composition: First year, first semester, three hours, 24 students per class section, Text: Roberts *Understanding English*: Concentrates on organization, principles of rhetoric, sentence structure, punctuation, etc. Material of themes is objective.

Speech: Second year, one semester, four class and three credit hours, 12 students per class. Text: McBurney and Wrage *Guide to Good Speech*. It builds on what the student knows, from Freshman English, of organizing materials — introductions, organizing and developing major units, transitions, concluding — and gives practice in applying rhetorical principles to various speech situations. Also stressed are elements of delivery, logical and psychological means of motivating an audience, and effective listening. Speeches are both extemporaneous and prepared, and subject handling both informative and persuasive. Subjects of speeches range from the technical through current political and social problems.

Technical Writing: Third year, second semester, three hours, 24 students per class, Text: Tuttle and Brown *Writing Useful Reports*. Here the general principles of writing are adapted to varied writing situations, being illustrated and practiced in various report, memorandum, and letter writing situations. Use is made of what the students have learned in Speech, especially in respect to motivation and to adaptation of material to the needs of the audience (reader). Movement of the course is from the more objective to the more "psychological." Stress is on using general principles flexibly, not on types or "formulas." This course also covers use of the library and finding, evaluating, and using recorded facts.

Masterpieces of Literature: Fourth year, first semester, three hours, 24 students per class. Texts: Perrine *Sound and Sense*, Speare *Pocket Book of Short Stories*, Barnet et al. *Eight Great Tragedies* (Mentor) and others. The course includes significant works from world literature, including poetry, drama, short stories and novels. In addition to the common texts indicated, each teacher selects three literary works he himself values and respects. All use one novel and most two (*American Tragedy, Tom Jones, Red Badge of Courage, War and Peace,* etc.) Most use an epic (*Divine Comedy,* Hell; *Paradise Lost; Iliad*), one uses biography (Ludwig's *Napoleon*). The course seeks to increase the student's appreciation of literature and its function in expanding his knowledge of human experience and himself. Since the student writes frequent papers, he now gets experience in expressing himself in non-technical areas.

In addition to these courses required of all students, electives are also offered. In Speech these include Conference Speaking and Advanced Public Speaking. In English they include Modern Plays, Short Stories, and Directed Readings (*1984, Gulliver's Travels, Utopia, The Republic*).

The Freshman course, then, is simply a first step in a series of expanding and increasingly complex experiences with the written and spoken word.

b. *Rationale*

The objective of the current freshman course is to help the student develop his skill in expository writing — that is, to organize material effectively; to express ideas clearly, exactly and objectively; and to employ acceptable practice in grammar, spelling, mechanics, and punctuation. The course can be thus limited because it is only the first of a series. The materials and approach are determined by four considerations:

(1)   The students aim to become engineers. Their interpretation of engineering being incomplete, their interest in the scientific, the mechanical, and the practical is both more intense and more exclusive than it ever again will be.

(2)   The plant interest in good coordination reports and the obvious importance of communication in the plants make it easy to motivate the student to want to write well. Skill in expository writing becomes clearly an important professional tool.

(3)   Subject matter and expository writing assignments which recognize "where the student is" will be most likely to call forth his best efforts.

(4)   However, the assignments should not be of the "formula" type. For example, he should not be given a pat outline of how to describe a process, which he then uses by "plugging in" his specific subject matter. Instead he should learn that all expository problems are met by flexible application of basic rhetorical principles.

(5)   Even in matters of sentence structure, mechanics, and punctuation, wherever principles or reasons exist, the student will be more likely to learn effectively if he learns the principles or reasons rather than simply the practice

(6)   The student must feel confident of reasonable success from the first. The course must therefore begin with simple assignments and relatively easy requirements for passing. However, requirements should increase rapidly enough that all will feel the necessity of continued effort, and that all will write competently by the end of the semester.

c. *Materials*

Materials include one text and "handout" directions and exercises. The text: Roberts *Understanding English*.

The handout directions:

(1) Objective, Procedures, and Grading Standards.
(2) Grading Symbols and Methods of Correcting Themes.
(3) Procedures for Writing an Abstract.
(4) Recommended Practice for Numbers and Abbreviations. The exercises (prepared in advance, several for each purpose, and used at the instructor's discretion) :

> Sentence recognition
> Kinds of connectives
> Sentence patterns
> Sentence structure
> Grammatical usage
> Punctuation

The Roberts text is notably effective in teaching sentence structure, punctuation, and diction, but not organization or rhetorical principles. Since all elementary texts using technical motivation for teaching rhetoric use a "formula" or "types" approach, none is now used, so that the teacher must provide appropriate guidance.

d. *Methods*

The course is flexible to the needs of the particular class and the judgment of its teachers. Thus the order of discussing topics, the particular methods, and so on, vary somewhat — but not as greatly as was expected when use of a common "calendar of assignments" was abandoned.

In each of the twelve weeks there is one writing assignment. After the first item, minimum word requirement is 300, but the average theme is well above 500. General topics are

(1) a developed paragraph
(2) description of a process
(3) description of a layout, giving reasons for the arrangement
(4) description of an organization
(5) description of a mechanism

(6) comparison of relative merits of two items
(7) an interpretation of data
(8) a summary abstract
(9) an expanded definition
(10) explanation of a classification
(11) establishing and justifying standards
(12) a critical evaluation using these standards.

An outline is required for each theme. Each fourth theme is written in class.

Early in the course the teacher discusses objectivity, outlining, methods of development, and transition. During the first twelve sessions he also handles certain material from Roberts: the orienting chapters, word classes, sentence recognition and sentence patterns, combined patterns, and intonation. In the second twelve sessions comes the material on expanded patterns, immediate constituents and sentence modifiers, and punctuation. In the final twelve sessions comes the material on diction and economy. All themes are given a "split" grade — above-the-line and below-the-line. The former evaluates organization and content, the latter grammar, sentence structure, spelling, and other mechanics. Both grades must be "passing" for the theme to pass, and both must average passing for the course. Otherwise, weighting of various projects is the concern of the teacher.

All themes are corrected. The correction symbols refer to specific numbered paragraphs of Roberts, or to certain supplementary material. The student is required to read the pertinent material, determine what part applies, and formulate a statement of why his effort was inept or of what principle he neglected. He then corrects the ineptitude. Good analyses and corrections modify the grade upwards, weak ones downwards.

The following, which uses traditional terminology, will give an idea of how "below-the-line" standards increase. (Numbers are numbers of the theme as listed above. All items are *marked* before the time indicated so that the student may get busy on them, but they are not penalized.)

(1) Poor page appearance, misspellings, sentence fragments, comma splice, run-together sentences, errors in tense,

number or case, faulty capitalization, confusion of adjective and adverb, lack of parallelism.

(2)   Comma and semicolon with coordinate clauses, use of apostrophes, illogical coordination.

(3)   Pronounce reference, mixed constructions, shift in point of view.

(4)   Incomplete comparisons, dangling elements, other weaknesses in sentence structure; non-standard practice in abbreviations or numbers.

(5)   Further uses of comma and semicolon, use of colon.

(6)   All other punctuation.

(7)   Conciseness, exactness of diction.

(8)   All other items of diction.

As was stated, methods of each teacher differ.   However, a typical week in the middle of the semester might run something like this.

Monday: Students turn in revised papers from previous week. The teacher states the nature of the new writing assignment. Class discussion is concerned with how the new paper (say, "description of an organization") could be organized.   The movement each time is from principles to the particular application.   ("We know various ways of opening the introduction.   What are possible approaches here?   Which might be suitable under such and such circumstances?   But suppose we had this different kind of reader?   Would the approach change? How?"   Or "How would you divide a subject like this? What might be another way?")   Before the hour is done, it is hoped, the student will have a pretty clear idea of various possible ways to organize the material and will know that there *are* alternative ways.   He will see that the plan is like the plans of earlier themes, in that it uses the same general principles, but that the specific subject matter has called for some modification of what was done previously.

Early in the semester, the entire hour will go to this assignment.   Later, as students become more proficient, less time is needed because they see the possibilities more quickly and make the new applications themselves.   Class time gained is spent on the Roberts material.   Specific theme subjects are controlled by the individual teacher.   They are of course varied from semester to semester and from class to class in order to discourage plagiarism.

Wednesday: Revised papers are returned to students, sometimes with brief comments. New papers are collected. The class hour is then given over to the Roberts material or to related or supplementary discussion of language or rhetoric, as seems desirable to the teacher.

Friday: Graded papers are returned. Two or three successful papers are reviewed. If any particular kind of awkwardness was fairly general, the specific themes are examined and better solutions worked out. Next are examined errors of sentence structure, punctuation, and so on. Ones already covered in class are shown briefly, as review; or if any particular one is common to a number of students, special attention is given to it. Other samples may be shown to use as a basis for discussing newly assigned material from Roberts.

About half the teachers use the opaque projector for showing the samples. Some project the actual student theme; others will have had the selected items typed on cards to minimize paper shuffling. Most mix the two techniques.

The other half of the teachers simply read the material to the group and put selected sentences on the chalk board.

2. *Experimental Shifts*

No experimental shifts are currently in progress, since the present course has just been reorganized as a result of two specific experiments:

a. *Use of structural linguistics to teach punctuation rather than conventional handbook material.*

To teach punctuation, two years ago, half of the teachers used Kierzek (traditional) and half used material prepared by Sumner Ives (structural). A common test was devised and agreed on by all the teachers involved. Results with the first group of students showed that where the structural approach was used, the students did substantially better. The traditionalists felt that the test might be faulty and devised a new one. When it was given to the alternate four-week group of students, the earlier results reappeared.

Twenty-eight groups averaging 22 students per group participated. Specific test scores showed:

Score Range	Percent in each range	
	Kierzek	Ives
40-69	28	23
70-79	29	25
80-89	31	41
90-98	12	11

The increased percentage in the 80-89 score range was reasonably consistent throughout those classes using the Ives approach. And since 13 teachers were involved it seemed unlikely that the seven who used the structural approach would be consistently better teachers.

b. *Use of some non-technical materials, plus exclusive use of structural approach.*

In the fall of 1958, two classes were set up (i.e., four class groups of 24 students each). Since the Mathematics Department was also experimenting, the groups included students who had had high school mathematics through Solid Geometry and Trigonometry, and who had had B+ to A in all mathematics and English courses. After basic expository techniques were taught in relation to objective technical subjects, the essays in *Modern Minds* (Jones, Ludwig and Perry) were used as a basis for critical and imaginative writing. All language matters were handled from the structural approach. While the numbers involved were too small to assess statistically, general findings were:

> (1)   Range in student ability was not markedly different from that found in "unselected groups." This was not really astounding, since our "unselected" students will have had grades of B or better.
>
> (2)   About one-third of the students reacted negatively to the non-technical readings and theme subjects. Since in the Senior literature course the reactions on a scale of four showed 45 percent reacting in the most favorable category and less than one percent unfavorably, it seemed to confirm our belief that such reading and writing is best postponed to the time when the maturation of the student readies him for it.

(3)   Results in improvement of sentence structure, punctuation, and mechanics not only confirmed the earlier results in respect to punctuation only, but were even dramatic.   There was a two-thirds reduction of errors between first and last themes even though only the last theme was written "in class."   It seemed clear that we should use the structural approach consistently.

3.   *Changes by 1970*

There is some indication that the quality of preparation of our students is steadily increasing.   If the trend continues, and if the structural approach is used in high schools generally, it is entirely possible that the material of the current technical writing course (Junior) can be merged with that of the freshman course, releasing three hours for further study in humanities.

chapter 11

THE COMMUNICATIONS CENTER AT HAMPTON INSTITUTE

*Jessie L. Brown**

In 1941 the English Department at Hampton Institute was reorganized into the present Communications Center, which is designed to do three important jobs: "first, to help all students to read, write, speak, and listen effectively; second, to assist all students in understanding and appreciating the literary heritage of the world; and, third, to identify, encourage, and train young people who show promise of becoming superior teachers, graduate students, writers, actors, speakers, or speech correctionists." The freshman program in communication skills assumes primary responsibility for the first of these three jobs.

Four important assumptions underlying this program give some insight into the general philosophy of the college, common views held by the staff on the nature and teaching of communication skills, and the communication needs of Hampton freshmen.

1. Language is man's chief medium for thinking, understanding, being understood; and simultaneously it is an aspect of his behavior in social interaction.
2. The so-called basic communication skills — reading, writing, speaking, listening — are unique clusters of skills, sharing a common core of skills that integrate in the process of comprehending and conveying meaning.
3. Accurate, discriminating use of language forms and structure not only clarifies meaning, but improves the social effectiveness of the user.

*Professor of English.

4. Developing skill in communication is significantly related to the individual's concept of self and of his role in the culture.

In its earliest statement of objectives Hampton Institute committed itself to a program in which learning and living are concomitant in the educational process. The phrases that have through the years symbolized this philosophy are "education for life" and "learning by doing." The college is itself a community of about 1200 students and 140 faculty members and their families. In general, faculty maintain permanent residence in faculty homes. This is a community with a program of activity that is carefully planned each year to give students a heightened sense of their individual worth, social significance, and community responsibility. In the meantime, it serves as a laboratory for projecting and evaluating the learning that is being initiated in the classroom.

The communication program for freshmen makes use of the opportunities in this environment for live experiences in reading, writing, speaking, listening. There are six class-related community activities in communication: (1) The *Hampton Script* (a student publication), (2) The College Debating Society (Annually the society debates the British Debating Team, participates in intercollegiate tournaments, and last year instituted an annual tournament at Hampton Institute.), (3) The Radio Club (a script-writing-broadcasting group, producing programs for the campus), (4) The Speech Choir, (5) The Creative Writer's Group, (6) The Hampton Players. In addition, throughout the year freshmen attend two lecture sequences: (1) All College Assembly, featuring student, faculty, and off-campus speakers, (2) The College Lecture Series, featuring eight professional speakers who have achieved eminence in fields of particular significance to college students. Speakers of the lecture series usually spend several days on campus discussing their fields of interest with student groups.

Students are also encouraged to participate in a variety of voluntary, non-class related communication activities. Early in the school year each freshman begins keeping an inventory of his school-community activities by listing those he participated in while in high school and those he thinks he would like to participate in during college. We use this information to assist students in selecting activities and to relate our teaching more directly to the life-centered needs and interests of our students. The inventory, which is kept up to date through the student conferences, becomes a part of the student's record. To facilitate informal communication between the individual student and his instructor, each staff member reserves a minimum of six hours a week for the student conference, which is held by appointment.

The more formal content of the program is offered in three courses: Remedial English 100 (three or six hours, no credit), Written Communication 101-102, (six credit hours), and Oral Communication (four credit hours). We teach written and oral communication in separate courses because we feel that this arrangement permits more detailed instruction in the fundamentals that our students need than we are prepared to offer in a single course. An important consideration for us is that in this arrangement only persons professionally trained in speech teach the oral communication course. We attempt to take advantage of this differentiation without sacrificing integration of the student's learning. The students take these two courses concurrently for the entire year. They make use of common readings; periodically they have a common assignment to develop a topic into a speech that is presented in one class and into a written composition in the other class. Conversely, in the speech course, students are encouraged to write their most effective speeches after the effectiveness has been tested with an audience, while in the writing course they are encouraged to "talk out" a difficult theme before writing it. These assignments are especially valuable in helping students distinguish differences as well as similarities between oral and written speech.

Course Procedures and Description

Entering freshmen are placed tentatively in Remedial English or in homogeneous sections of Written Communication, according to grade placement on the California Achievement Tests in reading and language. During an exploratory two-week period in class they write two themes that are rated proficient or non-proficient on a writing proficiency scale developed by the staff, and in some cases students are retested on alternate forms of the California Tests. After we have reviewed the records of the students and observed their responses in our classes, we make whatever placement changes seem advisable. About one-fifth of these students are required to take Remedial English; about one-third of those taking it pass the course after one semester, and another third pass after two semesters. Those who do not pass enter written communication conditionally, if they are permitted to return in the fall. These students have proved to be poor risks, not only in the communication program, but in the college.

Eleven of the fourteen instructors in the Communications Center teach in the freshman program. Cooperatively we develop course outlines and materials, select textbooks, evaluate student achievement, and revise the program. At the beginning of classes each student receives a copy of the course outline consisting of objectives, an analysis of content, a weekly assignment schedule, standards of evaluation, and supplementary reading lists.

The common texts for the three courses are a current collegiate dictionary and a collection of essays, *My Life, My Country, My World*, co-edited by Dr. Hugh M. Gloster, Chairman of the Communications Center. The essays present mature thinking on problems directly related to the needs and experiences of college students. Beginning with titles of immediate concern, such as "If I were a Freshman Again" by Thomas Arkle Clark and "What Every Freshman Should Know" by Roger Holmes, the range of interest gradually expands to world issues, such as the United Nations and problems of South Africa. The essays provide a common background of thought to be explored through speaking, listening, writing, and further reading. Reading comprehension exercises, vocabulary study of words in context, and suggested topics for speeches and themes follow each essay.

Remedial English

The outline for the course gives the following orientation:

Remedial English is especially designed to give you assistance in overcoming your handicaps revealed by your entrance examination in reading and writing. Your instructor will work with you in class and in individual conferences in such a way that you can progress at your own rate of speed. It is assumed that by hard work and serious application of what you learn you will be prepared to enter the regular written communication course at the end of one or two semesters. The primary objective of this course, then, is to help you with basic tools of communication.

The most immediate problem at the beginning of this course is to get the students to feel they have something to say that is of significance in an English classroom, for, in their opinion, English teaching and sincere expression of their ideas have virtually nothing in common.   Therefore, for the first two weeks, with the exception of the exploratory theme, they talk about themselves and language — about observations they have made of users of language and levels of usage, about satisfaction and frustration they have experienced in using language, about previous language experiences in the classroom and in community activity.   Some of these students report never having composed a piece of writing in high school; many report having written not more than three papers. In general, they have concluded, from instruction, no doubt, that correctness of form governed by "the rule" is the chief, but unattainable objective of language teaching.   Throughout the discussion the instructor tries to initiate the student's re-education in the use of communication skills.

The content of the course is organized into three units: (1) understanding and observing standard English, (2) understanding structure and form in standard English, (3) using standard English in written communication.   In the first unit students read assigned essays, doing comprehension and vocabulary exercises.   Instead of writing themes, they write paragraph summaries of each essay. Emphasis is placed on the use of the dictionary, multiple meaning, and meaning in context.   In the second unit they study grammatical structure by building sentences instead of analyzing them, grammatical form in relationship to levels of usage, punctuation in relationship to structural elements.   Although students are assigned workbook exercises, which are corrected, their learning is evaluated by the grammar in writing.   During this unit they revise the summaries of the first unit, paying particular attention to parallelism and subordination.   An alternate form of the standard test in language skills is given at the end of the unit.   During the third unit the students write and rewrite.   Instruction during the second semester is largely tutorial, the content remaining essentially the same as that of the first semester.

Written Communication

The outline for Written Communication begins with the following statement of objectives:

English 101-102 is primarily a course in written communication. It embraces much more, however, because good writing is dependent upon skill in reading, knowledge of and facility in the use of words, command of a variety of language forms, ability to find and use materials, and skill in putting ideas together clearly, forcefully, and interestingly. The objective of the course, therefore, is to help you become more thoughtful, accurate, and convincing in your communication. To attain this objective, you must strive zealously to achieve the following aims:

1. To appreciate the significance of communication in human affairs.
2. To recognize the interrelationship of reading, writing, speaking, listening.
3. To evaluate your personal needs and progress in the course by your daily performance in recognizing and meeting in-class and out-of-class challenges in reading, writing, speaking, listening.
4. To improve your ability to read with understanding, good judgment, and enjoyment.
5. To speak and write in well-developed, meaningful sentences.
6. To write purposeful, fully-developed paragraphs and papers.
7. To apply a knowledge of descriptive standard grammar, usage, and idiom in such a way that meaning is clear and exact and the expression of meaning is conventionally acceptable.
8. To use words discriminatingly according to their meaning in context.
9. To spell accurately all words in written context.
10. To punctuate and capitalize accurately according to meaning, observing also arbitary forms of good taste in the conventions of writing.
11. To develop basic skills in defining and limiting a problem, then gathering, digesting, and using information pertinent to it.

The basic textbooks are a handbook on modern English, a book of essays, and a collegiate dictionary. Periodically, the department purchases for class use copies of a single issue of magazines such as *The Reporter, Atlantic Monthly, Saturday Review.*

Classes receive an extensive reading list from which they must read a minimum of three autobiographies and three novels.

The students' most important activity in this class, however, is writing bi-weekly themes (300-450 words), an autobiography (1200-1500 words) in the latter half of the first semester, and an investigation paper (1500-1800 words) in the latter half of the second semester.

In general, the students' reading-writing process involves five steps: (1) studying and discussing an assigned essay with a view toward arriving at a sound interpretation of the author's purpose, meaning, and implications; (2) reading independently on the same subject to examine contrasting purposes and views of writers attempting to reach different audiences; (3) planning and writing a theme on the subject for a specified audience, usually the class; (4) reading and discussing their themes to see if the ideas they attempted to put on paper succeed in getting off paper; (5) correcting and revising returned themes after having studied the instructor's comments and correction symbols.   In conference with his instructor the student reviews his progress and receives tutorial assistance.   Superior themes from all classes are submitted to a staff committee that selects a theme-of-the-month that is featured on bulletin boards, read and discussed in classes and sometimes published in the *Hampton Script*.

Oral Communication

The course outline begins with the following statement:
    English 103 is a course in oral communication. It is a great deal more than its title implies, however, because of the numerous opportunities and responsibilities that speech holds for us — in speaking and listening in countless, ordinary, day-to-day conversations, and in meeting with competence the many public situations which impose social demands on us as speakers, listeners, and observers.   Your goals in studying speech, therefore, are to become a more effective person, develop a better command of facts, learn to think more clearly, be more self-confident, and improve your habitual oral skills.

At the end of each semester, in addition to the written examination, the student takes a speech proficiency examination before his class.   This examination is rated independently by two speech instructors; the student passes the examination when both instructors have rated him proficient.

The content of the course is organized into six units: (1) importance and essentials of effective speech in a democratic society, (2) physical mechanics of speaking, (3) voice production, (4) responsible leadership and participation in group discussion, (5) motivated sequence in speech planning, (6) five basic types of speech according to speaker's purpose. Listening is treated as essential end of the speech communication cycle. An example of this may be seen in its role in three types of group discussion — round table, symposium, panel. Each student serves as a leader in at least one of these and as a participant in all three. The discussion is presented by the group to the entire class while the class listens and takes notes on content. Following the presentation the class participates in informal discussion, seeking further clarification or the extension of ideas developed by the smaller group.

During the first semester, preparatory to speech making in the second semester, the class analyzes speeches heard in the College Lecture Series; on occasion they meet in special sessions to hear on radio or television live speeches of national or world importance; and each student listens independently to recorded speeches in the Communications Center library. The content of a student's discussion and speeches is closely related to that of his reading and writing.

Experiment and Perspectives

An experimental program that began three years ago and has more recently progressed to its second stage of development is the focal point of interest in the freshman communication program. In 1956 entering freshmen with superior ratings on the American Psychological Examination, and the English placement tests, including the departmental examination on written composition, were exempted from the first semester of communication. In 1957 and 1958 students of similar rank were placed in special sections of Written Communication 102 in which the instructors were free to plan with the class both content and methods that seemed best suited to their needs. The trend of the course method has been toward independent study and seminar sessions. The general topics of investigation have been general semantics, opinion and persuasion, mass communication media, prose diction and style. The students and the instructors who have participated in the project have been enthusiastic about their experiences, and the students have maintained their superiority in college academic standing.

Last year we began the second phase of the experiment in cooperation with three selected high schools in the two immediate cities. High school students with superior academic records, including English, who made superior ratings on the tests used by Hampton Institute for advanced placement in communication, took the college written communication course instead of twelfth grade English. Their high school English teachers, working with an instructor in the freshman program, who served as consultant, used the college texts, course outlines, and tests. In the spring the high school students took alternate forms of the examinations by which they were selected. Those who have passed the course with an average of *B* or *A* and who have superior examination ratings in comparison with entering freshmen will be admitted to Hampton Institute with course credit in written communication. This fall selected high schools in three other cities are expected to join the program.

Still another aspect of this program is the Pre-College Session of summer school, in which unselected high school graduates throughout the country may enroll in the written communication course. Those who pass receive credit at Hampton Institute upon admission in the fall. Those who do not pass usually are better prepared to do the work required in freshman English wherever they are enrolled. Forty superior high school students throughout the country received Danforth Scholarships to participate in this program. The experimental work with the local high school English program is a part of a broader experimental program that is being conducted by Dr. William H. Robinson, Director of the Division of Education at Hampton Institute.

The information that has been collected in these developments suggests that within a few years we shall have evidence to guide us in the reorganization of the freshman communication program. Already several indications are apparent. It is highly probable that by 1970 the following major changes will have been effected:

1. There will be no Remedial English.
2. The content of the written communication course will consist of facts about language. The method

will be largely an adaptation of the independent study program.

3. Oral Communication, relieved of some of the responsibility of teaching fundamentals about communication, will become more of a laboratory course in which freshmen and upper class students work together on practical projects that they are participating in out of class. Students are requesting more assistance in preparing for television appearances, leading college vespers, assuming leadership in national student organizations, or making seminar presentations. With greater opportunity to exercise their abilities, superior students are becoming more aware of their needs.

4. The study of French and German, now electives for juniors, will be taught in the freshman program; Spanish will be offered and — we hope — Russian and Japanese. Rapid development in linguistic study, the prospects of language programs in the high schools, and the international composition of our faculty should afford us the opportunity to prepare our students for better communication in the world community.

Plans and hopes for the future, however, are sobered by our awareness that we must try to keep a clear vision of the limitations as well as the potentialities of each in-coming class. Many among them will have to wrestle with the perennial problems of literate reading, writing, speaking, and listening. The closing of public schools and temporary make-shift private schools in the South, from which most of our students come, along with over-crowded classrooms throughout the country, are stunting the normal educational growth of prospective Hampton students. Perhaps our strongest desire should be for greater knowledge, imagination, and dedication among the staff that will teach them.

chapter 12

THE COMMUNICATION SKILLS PROGRAM AT THE STATE UNIVERSITY OF IOWA

*Carl A. Dallinger**

Philosophy

Since 1944 the State University of Iowa has had a Communication Skills Program which presents the basic work in writing, speaking, reading, and listening in integrated courses at the freshman level. Faculty action at the time of its inception directed that:

this program should attempt to provide the degree of skill in writing, speaking, and reading that is necessary for effective participation in both college and non-college life, and furnish a basis for subsequently increased skill in these respects as knowledge and experience are enlarged[1]

This philosophy, with listening added as understanding of and interest in this aspect of communication has grown, has characterized the program since its beginning.

A core of rhetorical principles applicable to speaking, writing, reading, and listening provides the basis for integrating the teaching of these skills. Recognizing the reciprocal relationships between writer and reader, between speaker and listener, courses are organized around the concepts of: (1) purpose in discourse, (2) organization of ideas, (3) support of ideas, (4) reasoning, (5) use of language, (6) adaptation of the discourse to the communicative situation. Although the focus has been on integration, the unique

---

*Coordinator of the Communication Skills Program.

[1]*A College Program in the Communication Skills* (Dubuque, Iowa, Wm. C. Brown Company, Publishers, 1947), p. 5.

aspects of each of the four skills have not been overlooked —
paragraphing, punctuation, spelling, mechanics in writing; voice,
articulation, pronunciation, bodily action, adjustment in speaking;
rate, eye span and movement, skimming, and like techniques in
reading; factors which distract, note-taking, and similar aspects in
listening.

Although the study and application of these principles provides the basis of integration in teaching in the program, the emphasis in courses is on the acquisition of skills rather than on
content.   A basic level of proficiency as demonstrated by actual
performance in writing, speaking, and reading is required of students who exempt themselves from Communication Skills by test
upon matriculation at the University, or at the end of the course.
Students failing to meet the performance standard are held for
additional work in Communication Skills until an acceptable level
of skill has been achieved.

Recognizing that students come to the University with widely
varying abilities in communication, adaptation to individual needs
and abilities is provided through tests by which students of superior ability in communication skills can exempt themselves from
the requirement, and through accelerated, regular, and special courses
for students possessing varying degrees of ability and difficulty
in the communicative skills.   Students who exempt themselves from
the Communication Skills requirement by tests are not given college credit; they are simply permitted to enroll for other, more
advanced courses.   On the other hand, a limit of eight semester
hours is set on the amount of communication skills credit a student
can present in meeting requirements for a degree.

The Communication Skills Program provides the basic instruction in writing, reading, speaking and listening for all departments
and colleges of the University.   There are no parallel or com-
peting courses offered.   Satisfactory completion of the work in
Communication Skills or its equivalent by transfer of credit from
other institutions of higher learning is an undergraduate degree
requirement of all colleges in the University.

Because the program emphasizes those communicative skills
students will need in pursuing college work and in adult life,
expository, argumentative and critical writing and speaking are
stressed.   More advanced, artistic forms of discourse, such as stories,
poems, plays, are not included in the assignments.   Students are

encouraged to take advanced courses in writing, speech and drama, and to participate in activities which provide experience in these areas, but instruction in Communication Skills is not extended to these more advanced, artistic forms of writing and speaking.

Administration and Staff

From its inception in 1944 the Communication Skills Program has been a non-departmental instructional unit in the College of Liberal Arts. It is not in the English or Speech and Dramatic Art Departments. The work in Communication Skills is organized and directed by a Writing Supervisor, a Speech Supervisor, and a Reading Supervisor, one of whom functions as Coordinator of the Program. Administratively they are directly responsible to the Dean of the College of Liberal Arts. The policies and academic offerings of the Program are under the jurisdiction of the Educational Policies Committee and, through this committee, the faculty of the College of Liberal Arts.

The staff is drawn largely from the English and Speech and Dramatic Art Departments, with the Reading Supervisor and his assistants, who staff the Reading Laboratory, coming from the College of Education. Although a few classes are taught by regular members of the faculty, the majority of the staff members are carefully screened graduate students in English, speech and dramatic art. All but a few of them are Ph.D. candidates holding instructorships or teaching graduate assistantships.

Securing instructors competent to handle all phases of instruction in Communication Skills is one of the problems such integrated courses present. To the extent it is possible, appointments are made from candidates who present training both in English and speech, and who have had previous teaching experience. In addition, weekly staff meetings are held to provide in-service training on the teaching and evaluation of skills in writing, speaking; reading, and listening. Experience and research indicate that major instructional differences are minimized by this procedure and are largely eliminated after a year of teaching experience in the Program.

Testing and Sectioning

Students are sectioned in Communication Skills on the basis of tests included in the battery of University entrance examinations.

Prior to 1958, included in the battery were an English composition test covering grammar, mechanics, and usage, a reading rate and comprehensive test, and a vocabulary test, all of which were objective, machine scored. In addition, each student wrote an expository theme of at least 450 words and gave a four minute argumentative speech. Each theme and speech was rated by one or more staff members. Students were also checked for speech defects and were referred to the Speech Clinic if they were found to stutter or if they had voice and/or articulation deviations needing clinical therapy.

In 1958 a state-wide, college testing program was instituted which precluded the possibility of having all students write a theme and make a speech. Therefore, research was done to find a formula by which the objective tests could be so weighted as to give a sufficiently accurate prediction of a student's ability in Communication Skills to permit sectioning. Using as criteria of measurement the classification of students previously made on the basis of the full battery of tests, including the theme and the speech, and the course grades achieved by students in Communication Skills, it was found that the formula $Y = 6X_E + 3X_R + 1X_M + 3X_A$, in which X_E is the English Composition test score, X_R the Reading Comprehension test score, X_M the Mathematics Skills test score, X_A the Henmon-Nelson Mental Ability test score,[2] would provide an index by which students could be classified in Communication Skills with not more than 15% error. On the basis of this formula, students entering the University in September, 1958, were sectioned either in the one semester, Accelerated Course or in the two semester Main Course. During the first three days of the semester only the accelerated students (30% to 35% of the freshmen) were given theme and speech tests; from this group the exemptees (5% to 7% of the entering students) were selected. The two semester course students were not given the theme and speech tests and were not eligible for exemption from the course by test.

Students entering the University in September, 1960, will be examined by the interstate, American College Testing Program. These tests will be objective, machine scored, and will be similar to those used previously in the University entrance testing program.

---

[2] In applying the formula $Y = 6X_E + 3X_R + 1X_M + 3X_A$, if $Y = 816$ or above a student was classified as accelerated, if $Y = 815$ or below a student was placed in the two semester, Main Course.

For purposes of placement of students in Communication Skills, therefore, a formula similar to that used during the 1958-59 and 1959-60 academic years will have to be developed.[3] It is anticipated that the practice of giving theme and speech tests to the accelerated students during the first few days of classes and the selection of exemptions from this group of students will be continued.

Courses: Content and Final Testing Procedures

Beginning with September, 1959, the freshmen will be divided into three ability groups as far as Communication Skills are concerned: 5% to 7% will be exempted, 30% to 35% will be placed in one semester Accelerated classes, 60% to 65% will be placed in two semester, Main Course classes. Because students in the lower 50% of their high school graduating classes are now admitted to the university only after a careful testing of their abilities and appraisal of their records, the two credit Supplementary Course, which formerly was offered for these weak students in need of review of the fundamentals of writing, speaking, and reading, has been dropped. In place of the Supplementary Course, students who score at the 20 percentile or below on the English Placement test or the Reading Comprehension test will be referred to the Writing and Reading Laboratories for extra help in addition to their regular course work. The effect of this change will be to put the initiative on the weak students to make up their deficiencies; failure on their part to do so will increase their chances of failing in Communication Skills and in the University.

The courses concentrate on developing skills in expository, argumentative, and critical discourse. Emphasis is on performance, based upon the study of principles. The Accelerated Course telescopes into one semester the work normally covered in two semesters in the Main Course. It does so by assuming that the accelerated students have an adequate command of the fundamentals of writing, speaking, reading, and listening and are thus prepared

---

[3]On the basis of experience and additional research during the 1958-59 academic year, the formula used for classifying students entering the University in September, 1959 was revised to $Y = 7X_E + 3X_R + 3X_A$, in which X_E = English Placement test score; X_R = Reading Comprehension score; X_A = Henmon-Nelson Aptitude test score. For a Y value of 835 or greater a student is classified as accelerated, for 834 or less he is placed in the two semester, Main Course.

to concentrate on the organization and development of ideas and the more refined use of language.   If an accelerated student evidences a particular weakness that seems not to respond to the regular classroom instruction, he is referred to one of the laboratories for additional, individual help.

The first semester of the Main Course concentrates on the study of purpose in discourse, organization of ideas, and the use of good, specific material in the support of ideas.   At the same time that these matters of content are being considered, paragraphing, sentence structure, grammar and mechanics in writing are being reviewed; adjustment, control of bodily action, and basic aspects of voice, articulation, and pronunciation in speech are being developed; improvement in rate, and retention of main and subordinate ideas in reading and listening are receiving attention.   The second semester emphasizes the refinement of the skills covered during the first semester, the more sophisticated use of language, and the use of sound reasoning in the presentation and critical evaluation of ideas.

At the end of the course students take a battery of departmental tests, usually consisting of three objective tests: English Composition, Reading Comprehension, and a principles or vocabulary test. In addition, each student writes an expository or argumentative theme (450 word minimum) and makes a four minute argumentative or expository speech.   These performance tests are graded by two or three instructors.   A minimum level of performance must be achieved before a student is exempted from the course. Through the years an average of 15% to 20% of the students have been held for additional work in writing, about 10% for more work in speech as a result of the final performance tests.   Standards of performance in reading and listening have not been administered systematically in the past, but these skills will be incorporated more definitely into the final appraisal of the student's work.

For students who fail one or more of the final performance tests there are two-credit-hour, special courses in writing (in the Writing Laboratory), reading (in the Reading Laboratory), and speaking, for which a student must continue to enroll each semester until he achieves the required level of performance.

Research

Continuous study of the Program is carried on in an effort to evaluate and improve instruction. The most extensive, recent study, supported in part by a grant from the Fund for the Advancement of Education, was carried on during the 1957-58 academic year.[4] Recognizing the difficulty of obtaining instructors with adequate professional training in all of the essential aspects of Communication Skills and the attendant problem of teaching more students as college enrollments rise without a concomitant increase in well-trained staff members, this year of research was directed toward finding at least a partial solution to these problems. The following three methods of instruction in Communication Skills were compared experimentally:

> (1) the present method which makes one instructor responsible for the training of his students in all four skills (reading, writing, speaking, listening) ; (2) a method of teaching designed to make the student more self-reliant and independent by reducing from four to three the number of formal class meetings per week, by presenting the basic principles of the course, normally covered in lectures and discussion, in a bibliography of assigned readings, and devoting most of the class hours to performances under the guidance and criticism of a classroom instructor; (3) the presentation of the basic principles of the course by 'experts' through the use of film recordings of television programs (kinescopes), supplemented by discussion of these principles and their application in performance under the guidance and criticism of the regular classroom instructor.[5]

The following were some of the more significant conclusions resulting from this study. As measured by achievement on examinations, no significant differences between the three methods of instruction were found. Although the majority of the students and instructors preferred the present method of instruction, experience with the "bibliography" and the "kinescope" methods disposed students and instructors more favorably toward the method they had experienced. Achievement in Communication Skills was

---

[4] Becker, Samuel L., Carl A. Dallinger, Harry H. Crosby, and David Gold, *Communication Skills: An Experiment in Instructional Methods* (State University of Iowa, Iowa City, Iowa, August, 1958).

[5] *Ibid.*, p. 3.

significantly affected by instructor differences.   Except for speech,
". . . . students of greater general academic ability tend to do
better than students of lesser ability;" only students in the lowest
quartile of general academic ability were significantly poorer than
those in the upper three quartiles when rated on performance in a
four minute argumentative speech.   "The skills of communication
appear to have only slight relationship to each other, to knowledge
of the principles of communication, ... or to attitudes toward
communication."[6]   Although it was the least preferred of the
three methods of instruction tested, the 'bibliography' method of
instruction, which reduced the number of class meetings per week
and placed greater responsibility on the students to secure the
principles of communication from a bibliography of readings,
offers real possibilities where economy of staff and classroom space
are important considerations.

Because of a growing concern over the time and energy that
was being invested in the poorer students, during the 1958-59
academic year the supervisors of the Communication Skills Program made a careful study of the achievement of the students in
the lowest fifteen per cent in general academic ability.   From
1952-1958, only 25.8% of these students completed the requirements in Communication Skills in the normal period of two
semesters.   The remainder either withdrew from school, failed
the course, or were held for additional work in one or more of the
special courses for students who fail the final performance tests.
A carefully controlled study of the differences between normal
and poor readers in the Communication Skills Program revealed
that the poor readers were markedly inferior to the average readers
in verbal intelligence, the largest, single contribution to variance
between them.   Also, 46% of the poor readers were on academic
probation at the end of the first semester.[7]

As a result of these facts, formal course work for credit in
Communication Skills aimed at helping poorer students overcome
their deficiencies has been dropped.   Beginning with the 1959-60
academic year, students scoring at the twentieth percentile or below
on the entrance reading or English composition tests will be ad-

---

[6]*Ibid.*, p. 25.

[7]Hill, Walter Raymond, "A Multivariate Comparison of College Freshmen
with Adequate or Deficient Reading Comprehension" (Unpublished Ph.D. Dissertation, State University of Iowa, Iowa City, Iowa. 1958).

vised to do extra, non-credit work in the reading and writing laboratories; the initiative to make up his deficiencies has been placed upon the student weak in one or more of the communicative skills.

To discover whether one semester of Communication Skills makes a detectable difference in freshmen of superior ability, in September, 1954, the top two hundred freshmen, as measured by entrance tests, were randomly divided into two equal groups. One hundred were excused from all work in Communication Skills, the other group of one hundred took the one semester, Accelerated Course. The following May, all two hundred students were given the same battery of tests, with the result that the students who took Communication Skills were significantly superior on the English Placement test, the speech test, and the information test covering the principles of communication. Those who took the course were slightly, but not significantly superior to those who did not on the listening, reading, and theme tests.[8] Although this study sustained the value of instruction in Communication Skills for the superior student, the results were not persuasive enough to cause a change in the policy of exempting, on the average, the top 5% to 7% of the entering students as measured by entrance tests.

Future Trends

Certain directions for the future have already been set by research that has been done, by changes in college entrance testing that have been and are being instituted, and by the practical problems involved in servicing an increasing number of students. The course designed to help weak students make up deficiencies in the communicative skills has been dropped. Students below average in these skills will be expected to avail themselves of help provided in laboratories and clinics on a non-credit basis, while carrying work in regular courses. Those who cannot survive academically on this basis will be eliminated from the University. Instead of investing so much time and energy on poorer students, the emphasis is shifting to increasing the effectiveness of instruction for superior students. Since the beginning of the 1958-59 academic year, special sections in Communication Skills have been set up for

8"Communication Skills Exemption Study" (Unpublished, State University of Iowa, Iowa City, Iowa, May, 1955).

the superior freshmen in the Honors Program. Additional ways of adapting instruction to the needs of these students are being sought.

The mass testing of large numbers of students has already made impractical the inclusion of a theme and speech in the entrance tests. Because of the wide variation in the communicative abilities of students entering college, it will be very desirable to continue to adapt instruction to individual needs and abilities through exemption and placement procedures. However, it will be necessary to rely increasingly on machine scored tests for placement purposes, which means that we must seek for more accurate, objective measures of communicative abilities in students. In the Communication Skills Program at the State University of Iowa we have already experimented with the placement of students by means of objective scores, and have given theme and speech performance tests only to students classified as accelerated as a means of exempting the 5% to 7% who are superior in the skills of communication. Experimental testing will continue in an effort to find practical, educationally sound ways of handling an increasing number of students.

Swelling enrollments and a shortage of competent instructors will probably result in placing greater responsibility on the student for his own education. We have already experimented with the 'bibliography' method of teaching, which reduces the number of class meetings and makes the student responsible for securing his knowledge of principles through reading. Experimental results indicate real promise in this method. During the 1959-60 academic year we will experiment with a combination of lectures and proctored performance sections as a method of teaching Communication Skills. It is very likely that small classes meeting four periods per week will not survive the pressure of mounting enrollments. New patterns for instruction will have to be found.

The philosophy of an integrated course in Communication Skills at the freshman level has been accepted in the University community and should be the continuing pattern. The nondepartmental status of the program, administered by a Coordinator and Supervisors, seems to have provided a climate in which the courses can be well organized, developed, and adapted to changing conditions, and where research can be interesting and fruitful.

chapter 13

WRITING AT MASSACHUSETTS INSTITUTE OF TECHNOLOGY

*William C. Greene**

Since the time of the first world war the department which is now called the Department of Humanities has been charged with the responsibility of presenting some kind of liberal arts to the freshmen and sophomores of the Massachusetts Institute of Technology; since the second world war that department and the Department of Economics and Social Science — the two departments forming the greatest part of the School of Humanities and Social Sciences — have shared the liberal education of juniors and seniors as well. The question what of the total content of a liberal education to present in one sixth of a student's time, which is what the eight required semester subjects come to at M.I.T., cannot be satisfactorily answered. If one surveys, the survey must be very sketchy; if one works in depth, much, most must be left out. What node of integration of the diverse disciplines and subject-matters can be found if one hopes to bring many things to bear on one thing? Should the student be put through a planned curriculum or allowed to choose where to bear down from his own interest? The Department of Humanities and its predecessor, the Department of English and History, have for forty years — indeed for more than that, back far beyond this writer's ken — struggled with many of the possible compromises that these questions evoke. At the end of the first world war, largely under the guidance of the late Frank Aydelotte, a two-year curriculum was established: the history of Europe since 1815 in the freshman year as a basis for a sophomore

*Professor of Literature

year made up of a semester of political theory (Mill and Carlyle largely) and a semester of the social and philosophical consequences of Darwinism.   There were, of course, papers written and even public speaking practised in groups of ten.   There was little formal instruction in writing, though fairly careful criticism in individual conference.   There was somewhat more formal instruction in speaking, but, unfortunately, insufficient practice.   Various teachers, eager to broaden the subject-matter into other areas, established options in this scheme: literature, scientific method, current events, history of thought.   All these were regarded as materials with which to practice writing, but by now the time demands on teacher and student and the sentiment that an ill-done job better not be done at all forced the dropping of speech as a formal requisite, though for a while there were class reports, especially in recent history and recent literature where magazines were often the sources of material.

Then a sentiment developed in the faculty at large that more time must be spent on formal instruction in composition, and for some dozen years, perhaps, the freshman year was devoted, half or whole, to composition, the history course moving up to the second year.   A good many kinds of composition were tried, even, at one time and by the impetus of a since nationally distinguished figure, the odd trial to teach composition by the writing of patents (an interesting experiment in writing specifications with great exactitude and claims with the utmost allowable vagueness).   When, at last, the principles of logic from an optional course in scientific thought were made basic to composition, something like a serviceable and interesting way to teach M.I.T. students to write came into being.   Books of reading and rhetorics were given up; the students wrote, planned, outlined, syllogized, argued, judged out of their own experience and out of several "cases" put together (from the Congressional Record, in fact) as material to write all sorts of papers from.   The teachers had to understand, among other things, a few simple physics and chemistry experiments (and often felt the need to teach the freshmen what was going on in the labs) ; the purpose was clearly not the writing of scientific papers but the comprehension that the same sort of evidence, generality, and logic enters all sorts of writing.   The teachers of this course, however, graduated to other subjects, and then, at the end of the second world war, the whole scheme of humanities was altered.

It had been proved that composition could be not unsuccessfully and not uninterestingly taught, but many members of the Department of Humanities and of the administration felt that, in the limited time allowed for all liberal arts study, some organized humanities substance could better be the basis for composition. Thus there was established a new freshman year, devoted to the examination of present and past societies as seen in their history, drama, philosophy, poetry. The sophomore year was to be given to the history of the United States in the world and to, what was at first a smaller option, the history of ideas since, roughly, 1700. Student grades were to depend upon success in writing frequent papers, and the class discussion of issues was to lead to those papers.

This is the framework of what is known as the core curriculum still in being. The junior and senior years are given to some ten fields, in one of which the student chooses three subjects and in another of which he chooses one (for almost all engineers, introductory economics).

The junior-senior electives have proliferated until the catalogue of subjects is as great as that of the average liberal arts college (minus, of course, the usual college science subjects), and have absorbed the attention of the older professors. The freshman year is still one subject common to all. It has, of course, changed its emphases. Its sociological bent after two or three years shifted to a more definitely historical one; never to the "seamless web," but to the problems of change seen in the usual famous periods of European history. Because the new young historians scorn any but original documents, the reading became more and more that of "great books"; and perhaps because of the feeling that a first course should prepare for later ones and that the one major preparation should be the technique of reading, the emphasis lately seems to have shifted from books as illustrating the broadest sense of history to books as examples of how a historian or a philosopher or a dramatist writes. Out of this closer look at books and the way they are written the students may be expected to see the value of words and their relationships and so may pretty directly learn some bases of writing.

Some shift has occurred in the uses of composition as well. The originators of the core curriculum were largely men who had come out of the earlier work in composition, history, literature;

all had taught all; and this new curriculum was pledged not to teach composition any less effectively than the curriculum it succeeded.   As time went on, however, and the originators dispersed or took up work in the upper class subjects, the staffing of the core curriculum became a problem.   Historians seemed to fit the requirements best, though many of them have been alarmed to discover they must at the very opening of their careers discuss Sophocles' *Antigone*.   There have been philosophers, sociologists, art historians, literature men.   The last, of course, are supposed to know something about composition, though they may be no more interested in a freshman version of it than teachers of other training.   At any rate there have been few, if any, whose specific experience has been in the teaching of composition.   There is, of course, a comforting illusion that any doctor or doctoral candidate knows how to write and how to read.   The early impetus toward the teaching of composition — which, as many of us have bitterly learned, is an art of no mean size, complexity, and self-abnegation — has perhaps withered a little.   More emphasis has been put on knowing material, more on understanding the meanings of books; perhaps the final examination has been given more weight.   Probably the average number of papers required has gone down from ten or a dozen per semester to four or five for freshmen and to two for sophomores, although some of the teachers insist on a paper a week and spend quite as much effort thereon as on the elucidation of books.

Over the last dozen years there have been many attempts to arrange some progressive series of papers, simple descriptions or reports, to explanations, arguments, judgments of value, and to show the kinds of material each of such papers will require.   One may begin, say, with a paper on what the character Creon in *Antigone* does; few freshmen will count his entrances and exits or the number of his speeches or thin out his commands from his comments; but the next paper that comes naturally from reading and discussion (of *The Bacchae*) may be: "What do you think Dionysus stood for in Euripides' mind?" and the evidence will be of a very different sort and the need for hypothesis will be the new trick. Thus the subjects that it seems important to discuss and for the student to think about cannot always be fitted naturally to the bed of a series of exercises in composition.   One supposes that it is the more discursive subjects that are now in general assigned; the student, then, gets practice in writing papers whose theory comes to him somewhat helter-skelter. Yet in the process he will learn the need of evidence, principle, and logic and their place and use; though some of his teachers may grade him for having ideas, many will grade him for the way he uses the ideas he has, and this will make him conscious of composition as an art.

Since it has been, quite properly, felt that "bright young men," most of them with a doctor's degree or well on the way to getting it, would teach better and more happily if allowed considerable pedagogical freedom, there have been no hard and fast rules about written work and little control but the individual conscience. The fact seems to be that the individual conscience does operate; there are many young teachers who spend long hours over papers and long hours discussing papers with individual students. And there has been a compensating factor in the precedent training of the incoming freshmen, whose average verbal aptitude scores have risen in five years from 565 to 642; indeed, in the present freshman class there are very few below 500, very few, really, who need much training in the details of rank literacy. Thus in the whole setting of the job of the department the kind of composition practised, non-theoretical but carefully criticized, has proved manageable, flexible, and so far as one can tell quite as successful as the previous more formal instruction.

There are, of course, some ancillary efforts. Each freshman must now take one elective from a group of twenty or so; many, perhaps most, take two. The Department of Humanities offers three of these and reaches through them a quarter to a third of the first year students. One member of the department teaches a subject in composition; another a subject in public speaking; another, scientific method. The first two are, of course, directly concerned with communication; the third may, because it is some introduction to logic, help those who take it to better communication, but it is not thought of as serving that purpose. None of these are required; they are opportunities for the interested, and the interested are not always the needy.

Though every member of the staff of humanities at M.I.T. would admit that too little is done with writing in the first year, and far too little in the second year, the general opinion of the teachers is that the great majority of the students can make clear in correct form what they have to say. The greater problem lies in the subjects beyond the first two years and in subjects outside the humanities.   One suspects that at the good liberal arts college, even though there is little writing per subject, there is an insistence on good composition all through, and four or five papers a semester, though in different subjects and insufficiently criticized and corrected, offer some chance for practice.   In an engineering school, however, there is almost no practice in writing, outside the humanities and that not scientific — until a senior thesis comes along. At that point the thesis supervisor is inclined to scream, and quite properly, for the student, though he may have had one paper a term in his humanities subject, has never been instructed in or had practice in writing a technical paper, and if he has written exams, they have not often, one guesses, been marked down for faults in composition. (The impression here given is unfair, for there are any number of teachers in science and engineering who are as offended by bad writing as the most sensitive literary man; but they do not often find a way of evaluating bad writing versus right answers in the grade given, and the grade is where the rub comes for students.)

There is no question that the junior-senior humanities subjects must bear blame here.   Many teachers make valiant efforts; the teachers of the introductory literature course are turning toward the weekly paper on the new reading; one of them demands, for at least ten weeks of the semester, a paper a day.   But the term paper dominates, and it has, of course, its uses in persuading the student to do some research and thinking on his own.

What is the direction of the next dozen years?   Well, in a dozen years we shall still be saying that composition is important, that teachers in it are rare, that the fields elsewhere are far more golden.   If one says there are a million freshmen in American colleges and each must have composition, at the rate of one hundred students per teacher — and few of us would want really to teach composition to one hundred students at a time— the demand is for ten thousand teachers of composition, who must be intelligent, experienced, especially sensitive to each individual student, and willing to forego such glory as academic life offers.   The engineering schools can hardly expect to find their share of such teachers as there are, for there is somewhat less kudos teaching composition at M.I.T. than at Harvard, say.

The problem of composition, then, is one which it seems unlikely any sweeping plan or foundation grant will solve.   One must go on depending on the general literacy and conscientiousness of men trained in other disciplines.   One may try to help some of the juniors and seniors with courses in report-writing, as M.I.T. does, and with men trained therein open to consultation by students with problems, but it is M.I.T. experience that not enough department heads are willing to give time from the professional curricula to formalize such activities, — and the Department of Humanities is unwilling to sacrifice its brief hours for liberal arts to the technique of composition.

As this is being written, the School of Engineering has been given nine million dollars to reform the teaching of engineering education at M.I.T.   There is some sign that the reform will be not patchwork but all-over revolution.   If that comes about in anything like the shape some dreams of the moment take, a fair guess would be that a good deal more communication, oral and written, would be required of teachers and of students, more written analysis of situations and of tools, more projects and reports on projects.   It would seem unlikely that formal instruction in composition by the Department of Humanities would be asked for, but it would seem likely that more practice would be done and the ultimate goal of literacy more often reached thereby.   Indeed, the non-verbal engineer might well be unable to graduate or to perform the job of engineering, — as he is even today, though the incipient engineer is not aware of it.

The greatest boon to college composition, of course, would be the eradication of the need for it.   If in the field of composition something can be done like the already visible improvement in education in physical science in the high schools, that need may well for the great proportion of college students vanish.   Certainly the freshmen coming to M.I.T. in the last two or three years need less training in mechanics, even in organization, than they do in the process of thought, and the process of thought is the major subject matter, no more of their humanities than of their whole education.   With which this writer passes the obligation on to all other teachers in all other subjects, where in the long run it cannot escape finding its proper home.

chapter 14

COMPOSITION AND LITERATURE AT MIAMI UNIVERSITY, OXFORD, OHIO

*Gordon Wilson**

I. The Present Course

English 11-12, 15-16, Composition and Literature, three hours credit each semester, is the required course for freshmen in Humanities in the Common Curriculum. The probable enrollment in September, 1959, is 2230 students in 76 sections taught by 39 instructors of all academic ranks, Professor to Graduate Assistant. English 15-16, "For Advanced Freshmen," enrolls about 12 percent of the total class, selected primarily on the basis of the Total English percentiles in the Cooperative English Test. Its purpose is to recognize and encourage superior students by sectioning them with their peers and offering them an enriched program. There is no remedial program.

Purpose: The general purpose of the course is to improve the students' ability to make effective use of written English, to read and write effectively.

In English 11 and 15 the focus is on expository materials and techniques. In writing, the purpose is to develop the students' ability to write accurate and effective English in expository compositions. The compositions are reports and statements of opinion and formal arguments, the language is basically denotative, and the criteria are rhetorical and logical. In reading, the purpose is to develop the students' ability to read effectively informational, intellectual, or denotative works in several areas of knowledge. In

---

*Assistant Chairman, Department of English.

knowledge, the purpose is to equip the student through practice and instruction with the techniques of using language effectively. In attitude, the purpose is to develop in students a sense of the necessity of accurate and effective written English and to develop their sensibility to language and their sense of integrity in the use of language. The judgment of effectiveness and attitude is based on the language practices of the community in which the students now need to function, the college; and the immediate practical end is to enable the students to thrive in the college community.

In English 12 and 16 the readings are literary works. The general purpose of the writing program is continued, but the compositions are of two types: (1) critical exposition, in which the students apply literary criteria in the exposition of literary texts; (2) a paper of personal observation and experience in which students employ the language of literature, or connotative language. In the latter compositions the subject matter is not only facts and ideas, but the moods, emotions, and sense impressions of the writer, and the compositions are unified not only by logic, but by tone and theme. In reading, the purpose is to develop the students' ability to read literary texts; that is, to enable them to read critically, to approach a text with the appropriate criteria and to apply the criteria in analysis, interpretation, and evaluation. In knowledge, the purpose is to give the students criteria for the critical reading of literary texts and a critical experience of literary works read during the course. In attitude, the purpose is to develop in students a sense of literature as an important specialized form of communication, with a characteristic structure, use of language, and kind of knowledge; to develop in students a sense of the value of the concrete, immediate experience offered by literature; and to develop in them a critical sense of the difference between literature and pseudo-literature.

Materials: For English 11 and 15 the texts are a rhetoric, a reader, a course manual, and a booklet of freshman writing. A rhetoric is chosen in preference to such specialized texts as a handbook, a grammar, or a linguistic text because of an assumption basic to the procedures of the course, that the student entering college is equipped with a working language which varies from the most effective forms of standard English only in detail and in richness, and that the function of the course is to enable the student to make a more effective use of the language structure he already possesses. The procedures of the course are, on the lowest level, to bring his personal style into harmony with the forms of standard English, and ultimately to enable him to develop a rich and complex instrument for communication and expression. Obviously the rhetoric to be chosen is one which assimilates the attitudes and materials of recent language studies.

The reader for English 11 is chosen for the rhetorical effectiveness of its individual selections and for the range of the selections over several areas of knowledge. English 15 adds a specialized text in language and a source book for one of the reference papers.

In English 12 and 16 the literary texts are organized by types, a single text for English 12, and collections of individual types for English 16. Preferably, the texts contain a critical apparatus.

In English 11 and 12 and 15 and 16 semester tests are, in part, objective and departmental. The objective tests are multiple choice in type, and designed to examine the student on his knowledge of language, rhetoric, and literature, and to examine him on his ability to apply principles and criteria. Letter grades are worked out on the basis of the total class performance. On the minimum level they require that the student qualify in the area to pass in the course. A comparable test in fundamentals is given at the five-weeks' period in the first semester. Tests in composition are given at mid-term in both semesters and at the close of both semesters.

Currently the Vu-Graph is used as a means of class instruction. Beginning in September 1959 classroom instruction will be supplemented by weekly television lectures and demonstrations.

Staff and students are supplied with a course manual containing the program, statements of standards and procedures, and a style book. The English 11-12 Manual contains a daily schedule of assignments worked out, where possible, on a weekly-project basis. The English 15-16 Manual contains the same general matter as the English 11-12 Manual, but the schedule, divided into eight and five-week periods, is less rigid. In addition, both staff and students receive a regularly published booklet of exemplary compositions from the preceding year, which serves to indicate the type and quality of work done in the course. The staff also receives mimeographed sheets expanding the statements of purpose and objectives and describing in detail the purposes of individual writing assignments and the criteria for evaluating them.   There are regular meetings with new staff members and with program and examination committees.   Instructors hold a minimum of two formal conferences with each of their students each semester.

Methods: Instruction, readings, writing assignments, and tests and examinations are organized in a structure designed to accomplish the purposes of the course.   This structure of individual assignments and the whole course is published and distributed to both staff and students.

The fundamental process of the composition course is assigning and reading compositions.   In English 11 we customarily make one writing assignment each week.   In all assignments the focus is on the composition as a whole.   The form of each composition is the subject matter of instruction and assignment.   The whole process — lecture and demonstration, discussion of materials in rhetoric and reader — is intended to supply the student with the principles and the materials for the composition and the instructor with the criteria by which he will evaluate the composition.   The writing assignment is in the form of a subject-verb-complement statement as a controlling idea, or thesis, or statement of purpose. The assignment is not "free," whether the statement is framed by the student or the instructor.   Each composition is then an assignment in problem-solving; the problem is one in rhetoric, in effectively presenting materials for a rhetorical purpose.   In the progress of the course the assignments begin with the simple report and increase in complexity through definition and analysis to argument.   The criteria are cumulative.

An example of this approach is the assignment in analysis. Analysis is treated, not as a mechanical pattern into which material can be stuffed, but as a logical tool by which a certain kind of information can be discovered about a subject and represented in a composition.   The instructor uses the rhetoric to supply principles in the abstract and the readings to exemplify analysis as a logical process and a method of organizing a composition.   In the class exploration of these materials and the instructor's elaboration of the writing assignment, the student is given a problem in analysis and the principles and materials with which he will work.   The instructor judges the composition, first, by criteria from the assignment; that is, he evaluates it as an effective solution of the problem. He judges it, secondly, by the criteria for accuracy in form and by the criteria which have accumulated from preceding assignments. If the paper evades the problem of the assignment, it is not acceptable: the student has not demonstrated that he has learned what is being taught.

Of course, all compositions must meet the minimum requirement of accuracy; that is, the language must be in harmony with standard usage. Further, the instructor applies a constant standard; he judges the first paper and the last in the term by the same standards.

Half the compositions are written in class under test conditions. The first paper dealing with a rhetorical problem is a practice paper, written out of class, so that the student has a chance to revise and receive criticism. The second paper, written in class, is the test.

Matters of grammar, punctuation, spelling, sentence structure, diction, and vocabulary are dealt with in every composition, in context whenever context is important, in readings, and in assignments in the rhetoric. The rhetoric supplies knowledge and principles and exercises, but the study of these matters is conducted principally in the analysis of readings and the students' own writing, not in drill.

The readings in English 11 and 15 serve three functions: they are exercises in reading; they exemplify practices in composition; they supply materials for composition. As a means to an accurate and comprehensive understanding of what is said in informational writing, the student is given instruction and practice in (1) identifying the purpose of the writer, (2) stating the central idea of thesis of a composition, (3) writing a sentence outline of the major divisions, (4) identifying the organization or method of development of the whole composition, (5) identifying the topic sentences, methods of development, and the transitions in the paragraphs, and (6) identifying the major transitions in the whole composition. As the means to judging the effectiveness and validity of the composition, the student is given instruction and practice in evaluating the appropriateness of matters of organization and of diction, sentence structure, and details to the purpose of the writer, and the adequacy of evidence and logic and in the support of the writer's viewpoint, opinion, or argument.

The writing in English 12 and 16 is similarly structured, with the difference that the texts are literary and the papers critical expositions, and that the instructor assumes the students' competence in matters taught in English 11 and 15. The criteria for all compositions are cumulative from the first semester of the course.

In English 12 and 16 the purpose of the reading is to acquaint students with a body of literary texts and in the process to supply them with experience and with criteria which will enable them to read effectively on their own. The approach is critical in that the instructor deals with a play, poem, or story as a special kind of language structure with both typical and unique characteristics. By the process of explaining and asking questions, he leads students into an understanding of the work being read and equips the student with criteria by which he can read other works of the same type. As an exercise in reading and a test of the students' developing ability, the instructor regularly assigns for written composition problems of the function of elements in the literary work. These critical expositions are effective means of making all students participants in the class program, of making them active readers, and of supplying the instructor with tangible knowledge of student progress.

The tests in both semesters of both courses are largely problem solving compositions and objective tests composed of problem solving items. Half of the compositions are test papers. At midterm and at the close of both semesters, the tests in compositions are writing assignments so structured that the student must face specific problems in developing his composition. Students are prepared for these papers, as they are for all test compositions by guided discussion of readings during the class meetings preceding the tests. The instructor then gives the class two or three statements or questions from which one is chosen on the day of the test. The final examination in composition in English 11 is composed of three of these test papers over a period of three weeks. For each the instructor poses a different rhetorical problem so that the student is rather thoroughly tested in the light of the purpose of the course.

In addition to the tests in composition, objective tests on the principles and content of the course are given at the five-weeks' period in the first semester and at the close of each semester. The five-weeks' objective test is intended simply to identify and to warn those students whose knowledge of English fundamentals is inadequate. The objective, multiple choice test at the end of the first semester is intended to examine the students' ability to apply the principles of rhetoric which have been the subject of study during the term, and to examine their skill in critical reading. The test is composed of passages followed by a series of multiple choice questions in which students are required to make choices in diction, sentence structure, organization, transitions, and to identify and evaluate the process of composition and argument. For both of these tests, the subject matter is published in the course manual.

The final examination in English 12 and 16 is an objective, multiple choice test over the content of the course, with the emphasis on interpretation, and a similar test of the students' ability in the critical reading of literary texts. In the first part, the lead supplies information about a poem, story, or play read during the term, and the choices examine the students' understanding of the item. In the second part a poem, a story, part of a play, all presumably unknown to the students, are supplied and a series of questions on each examine the students' ability to make a critical reading. The objective tests are departmental and the grades are based on the total class performance.

Grades in the course are based on the student's performance in all the areas in which he is tested; but he does not pass the course until he qualifies in all the areas tested.

II. Experiment

In the spring of 1956 we began an experiment in large class instruction one of four various experiments on campus in the Experimental Study of Instructional Procedures under a grant from the Fund for the Advancement of Education. The experiment ended in the spring of 1959. Data for the first two years of the study have been published; the final reports should be available this fall.

The question we asked ourselves was, at the time, an urgent one: What do we do when the enrollment in the course is so great that we can no longer find competent instructors to staff the multiplying conventional sections? The possibilities of television were being explored elsewhere. We set ourselves to discover, within the conventional classroom and our current program, how effective a competent instructor could be with approximately twice as many students in each of his sections.

Since we regard the critical reading of compositions by an instructor who knows the precise assignments and also knows the student as a person — not merely as a signature — essential to our course, the increase of the paper load was the primary obstacle. In the experiment we reduced the number of compositions in the augmented or experimental sections so that the semester load equalled the semester load in the control sections. The control sections enrolled twenty-seven students who wrote thirteen compositions during the semester. The experimental sections enrolled forty-seven students who wrote seven compositions during the semester. During each year of the experiment, four instructors each carried an experimental and a control section, so that the measurements were of student performance, not of instructors' relative effectiveness. The problem of the instructors was to find instructional means by which they could accomplish as much in the experimental as in the control sections.

The structured course and careful control of the experiment made valid comparisons possible. In the pre-tests and post-tests in composition, reading anonymous papers unidentified as first or second efforts, two graders reached 90% agreement in overall grades. In general, the objective tests and the composition tests showed no significant differences in the performances of the large and the small groups. In the comparison of high ability students in large and small classes, and of low ability students in large and small classes, the result was the same: similar performance, no significant difference. Large class or small, low ability or high, seven compositions or thirteen, composition tests and objective tests in rhetoric and literature, the average improvement of the students did not vary. Pending the report on the data of the final year and on the instructors' reports, this is the conclusion on the experiment.

III. The Future

During the past ten years the trend in the course has been towards acceleration and enrichment. During the next ten the general objectives of the course will probably not change, but the materials and methods may be changed gradually by several elements operating singly or in conjunction.

First, scholarship in the language will undoubtedly affect the content and methods of the course in two ways: in new concepts and in the training of future instructors. Second, increasing educational costs may compel changes in the methods of instruction: such a possibility has already occasioned experiments in large class and television instruction and in teaching composition as part of a content course.   Third, a change in the kind of students enrolling in college may be an additional cause for changes in method.   Such a change can result from changes of admission policies by State colleges and universities and from such acceleration programs as the Advanced Placement Program in combination with the increase of college level courses offered in the senior year of high school, of off-campus centers offering college courses to high school seniors, and of junior colleges.   Finally, a great increase in enrollment with its attendant problems of administering a program and staffing sections may result in a radical change of the course.

chapter 15

COMMUNICATION SKILLS AT
MICHIGAN STATE UNIVERSITY, EAST LANSING

*Frederic Reeve**

It is not possible to describe the present course at Michigan State University without a brief description of Communication Skills as taught here for fifteen years. That course was designed to teach the four mutually interdependent skills of reading, writing, spelling, and listening simultaneously. In an attempt to integrate the skills, students were asked to read, discuss, give talks, and write papers in a single skills area (developing an idea, defining, reporting, etc.) recognizing through their efforts the common disciplines as well as the differences among the four facets of the communicative process. Listening and speaking were regarded as active processes requiring no less effort than reading and writing. Classes met five hours per week — the fifth hour being considered the listening laboratory — and students gave five speeches and wrote five papers per quarter. The texts were a handbook, a speech text, and an anthology of diverse readings. The philosophy of the course was utilitarian; its emphasis was upon the development of skill, and all types of discourse from simple reporting to argumentation were studied. Its aim was to help the student read and write effectively at a level appropriate to college educated men and women, and to understand and evaluate the writing and speaking of others, sensitively and perceptively. The skills were not taugtht in a vacuum: "Think, investigate and gather material before you write or speak" was the continual counsel. Speeches and papers were graded equally

---

*Professor, Department of Communication Skills, The Basic College.

for content and expression. The content of the course was infinitely various — a strength in Cleopatra — a weakness with us. The lectures in the listening laboratory covered the history and value of language, semantics, logic, techniques of persuasion — the gamut of material run in most such courses, most of it valuable and pertinent. The range in quality of readings in the anthologies (we used five in fifteen years) depended, of course, on the editors, who were men of sense, judgment and catholic tastes. The course was flexible and syllabus revisions were planned by the whole staff. It was a success, but not an unqualified one. Why change?

With one very significant difference, the present course is not the radical alteration which many have supposed it to be. That difference is the dropping of the formal teaching of speech which I shall later discuss. At this point a bit of recent history.

For the past several years Communication Skills has been strongly criticized by some members of the department, by some students, and by some other faculty members and administrators. This is not a unique experience for Freshman English and should surprise no one. Many careful studies of student and faculty attitudes were made. In order to strengthen the course, a "Course Enrichment Committee" was appointed in 1957 to work for one year as a clearing house and advisory group, charged with submitting a report for staff consideration. This committee's report delineated apparent problems and made a number of suggestions. Without going into great detail, I should like to outline these problems and suggestions.

The course content appeared at times to be diversified to the point of superficiality. Student papers and speeches, developed as types of discourse, frequently lacked substance. The students did not write as much as they should. The final examination, which counted 50% of the student's grade and which tested application of skill, was difficult to study for and disappointed many students and instructors. The listening program was thought to be weak in conception, and was inadequately developed in class, largely owing to student and instructor prejudice. The course did not seem to complement the other three general education courses (Humanities, Social Science, Natural Science) as effectively as it might.

Th greatest single difficulty was with the teaching of speech, which paradoxically was regarded by most students (and many instructors) as the single most effective part of the course. The

problem derived from two causes. One was (and is) the size
of classes (25 to 30) and the prospect of increasing enrollment
and a much more slowly increasing staff, perhaps even a decreasing
one. Five rounds of speeches a quarter consumed a disproportionate
amount of time. The second, a consequence of the first, was the
amount of time students spent listening to one another, time which
many felt might be more profitably spent.

The committee recommended a more unified and richer content,
units of the course to be content units not skills units (e.g. instead
of a unit entitled "Giving Directions" or "Persuasion" a unit on
the nature of language or one on censorship). Student writing
should be greatly increased, probably doubled. The examination
should offer a greater number of questions based on readings.
Formal listening training should be dropped. A number of suggestions, none of them conclusive, were offered regarding speaking,
but no specific recommendation was made.

In the spring of 1958 the head of the department resigned
to run for high political office and a new department head was
appointed. At this point a decision was reached at the administrative level to drop the formal teaching of speech. It was understood
that considerable class discussion and frequent oral reports would
give the students opportunity to express themselves. We do not
now pretend, however, that we are still teaching speech in any
formal way and we do not have a speech text. There was considerable staff protest and debate, but the department eventually voted
in favor of the decision.

A second administrative decision, quite in line with the Enrichment Committee recommendation and almost universally ap-
proved by the staff, was to offer as the basis for the teaching of
reading and writing a number of documents of the American heritage — important speeches, political essays, short stories, plays,
novels and poems. These serve three purposes. First, they give
the course a unified, continuous and enriched content, worthy in
itself, and providing interesting and substantial material for class
discussion and papers. Second, they offer a complement to the
Humanities course, a course in the history and culture of western
Europe. Third, they offer a variety of models of expression and
countless examples of usage, style, etc., appropriate to the teaching
of writing.

The above history and rationale is a necessary preamble to a description of the present course, as outlined on paper and as taught in several sections spring and summer terms of 1959.

The course was planned by a committee which held weekly open meetings in addition to its regular sessions and made periodic progress reports to the staff for their reaction and confirmation. This committee also met with members of the departments of history, English, political science and communication arts for their reactions and advice.

The purpose of the course as stated for the students in the introduction to the Syllabus reads:

> The primary purpose of this course is to help you to improve your reading and writing. Its secondary purpose is to give you an opportunity to broaden and deepen your awareness and knowledge of our American heritage. You will improve your ability to read by studying selected documents dealing with living issues of the American past and present. You will improve your ability to write by thinking and talking about these documents and expressing your ideas and reactions to them in a variety of ways.

The course consists of three quarters' work, ten weeks per quarter, four hours per week for a total of nine credits. Each quarter is divided into four units of approximately equal length. Students are expected to write at least once a week both in and out of class, and the equivalent of one and one half periods a week is devoted to the study of writing. The remaining time is spent in lecture and class discussion. Many instructors plan to give a five to ten minute written quiz two or three times a week, but each instructor may teach the course to suit himself. A series of weekly in-service meetings, sometimes in small groups, will offer a chance for the exchange of ideas. So much for mechanics.

The texts are an extensive anthology of significant American documents, a standard writing handbook and the syllabus. The syllabus sets forth the course content and reading assignments in outline form and provides a reading and writing outline of language objectives for each of the terms. In addition, each term the students buy one or two inexpensive reprints of novels or plays which comment significantly upon one or more of the units.

The course is not a survey of American history or literature, nor is it a course in American political or social institutions. It is a course in reading and writing using as its source material a number of literary, historical, social, and political documents. Though the twelve units are arranged chronologically, each is organized around a particular conflict or problem which remains significant. Nothing is read or studied for its historical significance alone. The readings are selected to answer two questions: What is an American? (Is there an American?) Why is America the country it is today?

The first unit, the introduction to the course, is called "America Through Foreign Eyes," and offers opinions of commentators from abroad as an invitation to the evaluation of our country. The second unit, "The Puritan Heritage," addresses itself to man's relationship to God, as Calvinist, Quaker, Separatist, etc. Jonathan Edwards, Hawthorne, Cotton Mather, et al, still speak strongly, and a close examination of the Puritan oligarchy, forbidding at first to most students, becomes highly interesting when accompanied by the reading of Arthur Miller's "The Crucible," the paperback for this term. The third unit, "Struggle for the Rights of Man," takes a giant step with Franklin from Boston to Philadelphia. Readings are from Franklin, Otis, Paine, John Adams, and Jefferson, among others, and an attempt is made to show that the philosophy of the Enlightment remains today the guiding body of principles for the liberal mind. The fourth unit, "American Renaissance," concerns the American growing aware of self — self-reliance, self-identification, self-consciousness. The important readings are by Emerson, Thoreau, Hawthorne, and Whitman. During this first term the student begins exploring the library, familiarizes himself with some standard reference works, and is introduced to a large reserve shelf of books related to this course. Library work continues throughout the course, longer investigative papers being required the second and third terms.

The second term begins with a unit on "The Frontier in American Life," from the first frontier of the New England wilderness to the shores of the Pacific. Readings range from Timothy Dwight through Davy Crockett to Thomas Hart Benton, and interpret life on the frontier, the character of the frontiersman and the effects of the great expansion upon American life and institutions, effects quite obvious today. The unit is something of a jolt to classes steeped in "adult westerns." The first outside reading of the term is Rolvaag's *Giants in the Earth*. (We envision changing outside readings from year to year according to what is available from the host of pertinent works.)

The second unit, "A House Divided," deals with the issues leading to America's second revolution, the Civil War, e.g. slavery, abolitionism, agrarian south and industrial north. Speeches of Calhoun, Webster, John Brown, Jefferson Davis, and Lincoln are closely studied. The catastrophic clash of arms is not examined, only the issues, still unhappily very much alive. The third unit is entitled "A Civilization on Trial" and begins with the industrial North ascendant. The conflict between factory and farm, the great industrial expansion, its human victims, the attempts to curb and reform and the attempts to justify — these are the issues. The outside reading which dramatizes all of them is Frank Norris's *The Octopus*. The study of this novel leads to the fourth unit, "The Rise of Realism," rooted in Howell's literary theories and evidenced by Twain, Harte, Bierce and Crane, among others.

The third term opens with the most difficult of the units and the most controversial, "The Impact of Darwinism." Under this generalized heading students read a series of philosophical essays, including selections from Ingersoll, James, and Dewey, which are quite abstract, somewhat abstruse, but consistently challenging. From Darwinism and its philosophical implications, we move to the second unit, "A New Literature: Naturalism and a Search for Values." Selections are from Dreiser, Anderson, Faulkner, Hemingway, and others of their distinguished company. The outside reading for this unit and the next, a natural bridge, is Steinbeck's *Grapes of Wrath*. The third unit is "A Civilization on Trial: Part II," which brings the agrarian — industrial conflict into the twentieth century: "The revolt from the village" and the answering protest of *I'll Take My Stand*; the industrial boom and bust of the Twenties and Thirties; the social reforms of the New Deal. The final unit is devoted to an examination of America's tremendous responsibilities in One World, albeit a world divided. The conflict between the isolationism of Borah and H. P. Fairchild and the wider vision of Wilson, Roosevelt and Wilkie is the subject at issue.

It is obvious that the units of the course are highly selective and that they have been chosen arbitrarily. We made the choices fully aware of many other possibilities and are open to suggestions as the course evolves. There will be changes. Some have already suggested choosing twelve contemporary issues and tracing them into the past. But until a year or two has elapsed, prediction is impossible.

Such is the course. The charge of superficiality may be made, but it can also be made for such courses at every stage from grammar to graduate school, and with some validity. To offset the danger we have tried to select whole documents, not excerpts. Students study intensively for content and mode of expression and write papers centered in the ideas that are embodied in these documents. So far, student papers and class discussions have genuine substance and the readings of the twelve units seem to speak with a living language to contemporary young Americans. But only two terms have at this writing (September, 1959) been taught. The instructors thus far engaged are enthusiastic.

When the structure delineated in the present blueprint is erected, then and only then, will it be possible to determine its strengths and weaknesses, and to assess whether or not the gain has been commensurate with the effort and justifies the changes. I feel strongly that it will be a much better house to live in, but the winds have not yet risen nor has the winter set in.

chapter 16

FRESHMAN ENGLISH AT MOREHOUSE COLLEGE

*N. P. Tillman and Richard K. Barksdale**

The Freshman English Program at Morehouse College is broadly designed to be a key service course for all Morehouse students. It is assumed that students who complete this course of study satisfactorily are assured of some degree of success in the College's upperclass curriculum.

There are two large areas in the program. These are the area of writing (or English Composition, as it is more commonly known) and the area of reading. A sustained effort is made to effect close articulation of these two areas; for reading and writing, it is believed, are cognate areas. Generally, students who read poorly also write poorly; and students who read with facility write with almost equal facility. Therefore, at Morehouse there is a tight academic and administrative liaison between the English Composition staff and the reading staff. One evidence of this is the fact that the sectioning in English Composition is determined by performance on a standardized test measuring reading ability. Moreover, the members of the reading staff are full-fledged members of the Department of English, and what is accomplished in the reading area is of vital concern to all members of the Department.

*N. P. Tillman is Dean of the Graduate School of Atlanta University and former chairman of the Department of English at Morehouse College. Richard K. Barksdale is Chairman of the Department of English at Morehouse College.

I. The Writing Program

At Morehouse College there are three levels of English Composition. On all levels a student must satisfy the course with a grade of C.

Level I provides a course of study for select students of superior ability, some of whom have been accelerated for early admission to college. The major objective of this level is to teach the standards of good writing; and good writing, it is believed, rests on three basic principles: correctness, clarity, and completeness. The following passage is quoted from the Prospectus currently being used in our Level I section:

> The writing phase of this course is founded on the hypothesis that, since writing and reading are so closely related and are complementary processes, a student more readily learns Correctness, Clarity, and Completeness by reading and playing the "sedulous ape" to writers whose works well demonstrate Correctness, Clarity, and Completeness. Therefore, analyses of these works, as well as close functional study of usage in the Handbook, will be made to the end of producing weekly themes that are correct in mechanics and usage, clear in thought, and complete in design.

To furnish the student with models of good writing, an extensive reading list is appended to the Prospectus. Each student is urged to learn to read creatively and critically so that he might find in reading a much-needed source for constructive recreation. On this Level, an attempt is also made to acquaint the students with the Great Books of the Western World and to teach them to use the *Syntopicon* of this famous set of books.

Level II of English Composition is broadly similar in content and objective to Level I, with the exception that Level I is restricted to first-year students of superior ability and efforts are made to make Level I work more rigorous and challenging. For instance, Level II students learn the standards of good writing by submitting weekly themes modeled on an extensive reading program, but they are not required to read in the Great Books or use the *Syntopicon*. Moreover, Level II students are selected on a different basis from those students assigned to Level I. Students assigned to Level II sections read on the 11th grade equivalent or above as determined by their performance on the Iowa Silent Reading Examination.

Although Level I students take this same test and must perform with comparable ability, other criteria of selection are used to determine that they are students of superior calibre.

Level III is the level enrolling the largest number of freshmen. Students who read below the 11th grade equivalent are assigned to this Level. Teachers on this Level attempt to achieve three broad objectives:

1. To teach acceptable English as determined by writers and speakers on the cultivated level of contemporary society.
2. To lead students to read with comprehension and with reasonable speed.
3. To help students to become aware of the relationship between thought and mechanics.

Since good writing proceeds from straight thinking and ample knowledge, reading exercises are presented in conjunction with some form of writing assignment. Similarly, exercises in speaking are also related to reading assignments, whenever possible. Finally, instructors are urged to use audio-visual aids whenever such aids will prove effective and beneficial.

II. The Reading Program

Ideally at present, practically all Morehouse College freshmen should receive some help in reading to improve their skills in this vital area of communication. Staff limitations do not permit this, and only those students who read below the 11th grade equivalent are assigned to reading sections. Roughly, seventy-five per cent of each freshman class falls into this group. These are divided into small classes of from fifteen to twenty students on the basis of their reading scores.

The principal objectives of the Morehouse Reading Program are:

1. To acquaint the student with his present reading status and to orient him with regard to the nature of the reading process.
2. To inculcate appreciation of "how we read" and teach him the factors which impede or accelerate this process.
3. To provide such specific emphases on reading skills as the individual case demands.

4. To extend and enrich each student's reading vocabulary.
5. To correlate reading instruction with related units of work in English.
6. To provide guidance in stimulating wide reading in different interest areas.

Various methods and techniques are used to achieve these objectives. For instance, the first objective is achieved by administering a silent reading test, an oral reading test, a visual screening test, and personal and reading inventories to each student. In individual conferences during the Reading Clinic Period these test results are discussed and interpreted for the student. Of particular importance is Objective No. 3. To achieve this objective laboratory periods are set up, and each student receives individualized instruction through the use of graded work-type materials according to his needs as revealed through diagnosis and performance.

The results of the Reading Program are encouraging and impressive. For instance, in September, 1958, 181 freshmen, or 77% of the new students, read below the 11th grade level. By January, 1959, this number had dropped to 120 or 51%; and by June, 1959, the number had dropped further to 77 or 33%. In other words, in September, 1958, only 23% of the freshman class read on the 11th grade equivalent or above; but by June, 1959, 67% read on the 11th grade level or above. This represented a percentage increase of 44%. Stated another way, students in the reading program gain, on the average, 2½ years in reading ability within a single semester; and, where ability is keen and application sufficiently rigorous, a student gains 3, 4, or 5 years in reading ability within a semester. Studies have revealed that students who improve in reading also show improvement in the content courses in the freshman year.

It is our hope to expand our offerings in Reading so that all freshman can enroll in a suitable course and so that we will be able to set up a referral system for upperclassmen who have reading problems.

Both the writing and reading phases of the course are carefully analyzed from year to year to see where they can be strengthened in content and method.

chapter 17

EFFECTIVE COMMUNICATION AT THE STATE UNIVERSITY OF NEW YORK COLLEGE FOR TEACHERS AT BUFFALO

*William D. Baker**

Buffalo State's general education course, Effective Communication, has had a provocative history. In 1951 a general education commitee appointed by the president of the College began six years of planning and discussion; in 1957 the eight-course program required of all students was begun. Two courses touch on territory often covered by communication or beginning language courses elsewhere: critical thinking and literature. To understand Buffalo's approach to communication, it is necessary to see that the course is one of several related to a broad spectrum of human behavior and knowledge. That critical thinking and literature are separated from communication and divided into separate courses is more a matter of administrative convenience than deliberate policy.

The critical thinking area, embraced in a freshman course called Ways of Knowing, includes a direct and systematic exploration of a variety of ways of answering the question, "How do you know?" Such topics as empiricism, pragmatism, scientific inquiry, authority, skepticism, rationalism, and religious revelation find a place in this course.

The junior course in literature considers the thinking sequence in the development of the ideas of man as referred to in his literary heritage. It considers such ideas as man's idea of the individual

---

*Director, General Studies Division.

(including heroism), of God, of love and friendship, of good and evil, of society, (including progress) and of nature.

According to the college catalog, the communication course sets the following ideals for students: "study of the materials and purposes of effective communication and the symbolic nature of communication devices: mastery of the tools of communication (spelling, enunciation, punctuation, vocal inflection, grammar, pronunciation, interpretation of visual and aural media); analysis of techniques used to evaluate mass media."

The outline of the two-semester course, which is developed in much greater detail in the staff-produced teacher's guide (syllabus), is as follows (each sub-unit includes at least one writing, speaking, reading, and listening assignment):

I. The Nature of Communication

1. *The Process of Communication* (linguistic and non-linguistic processes; the psychology of communication; the place of ideas and symbols in communication). 2. *Language and Communication* (the nature of language, language change, how language symbols affect attitudes, denotative and connotative meanings). 3. *Purpose and Organization in Communication* (putting ideas together in an organized fashion; how to analyze the audience; the variety of ways of developing ideas; distinguishing between major and supporting ideas). 4. *The Content of Communication* (the materials of communication — facts and ideas; distinguishing facts from inferences and opinions; ways of identifying and evaluating ideas; the processes by which facts and ideas are derived from experience, the techniques of library study and research).

II. The Functions of Communication

5. *Defining and Analyzing* (the variety of ways of making meanings clear; the values of definition; defining operationally; the vocabulary of definition-context, denotation, connotation, *etc.*) 6. *Demonstrating and Explaining* (the nature of these processes, use of body motion, and gesture; use of visual aids). 7. *Reporting* (the nature and the uses of reports; distinguishing between a report and a judgment; how to select and limit subjects for investigation). 8. *Persuading and Problem Solving* (distinguishing between rational and irrational appeals; the techniques of persuasion; implications and uses of propaganda; implications of opinion in the persuasive

context; developing standards of evaluation and means of analyzing persuasive materials; approaches to problem solving).

III. The Applications of Communications

9. *Listening and the Mass Media of Communication* (types and methods of the mass media; the impact of mass media on society; the purpose and significance of each of the mass media; standards of evaluation of each). 10. *Reading and the Mass Media of Communication* (the nature and objectives of this unit are described in the previous unit; this unit differs only in that it concentrates on those media which call for intelligent and critical reading — books, newspapers, magazines, periodicals).

Although there is strong administrative support for the course, there is, happily a healthy critical concern about it. Some staff want better performance from students (grammar, spelling, diction, enunciation); others want more content (for example the elements of the artist's world — line, color, design, shape, *etc.* — as communication). To meet both proposals the staff searches for improved methods of teaching, and, gallantly, does the best it can with a fifteen-hour teaching load (not more than nine of which may be communication) and twenty-five students per communication class.

The staff reaches out experimentally to find new and better ways of accomplishing its end. The following "experiments" have been tried between 1956 and 1959 with some success.

Experimental Approaches

A number of *combinations* of courses have been tried experimentally. One teacher, for example, has combined the basic social studies course (Man and His Institutions) with Communication. Instead of meeting each course for three separate one-hour periods per week, he meets them together for three two-hour periods, integrating wherever possible the subject matter of the social studies course with the skills and applications of the Communication course. He did this for two semesters and kept the same students for the entire academic year. He found a gain in the two areas in which one would expect to see increased effectiveness; the written work seemed to be a cut above the usual and the debates in the social studies area seemed to be more prolonged and fruitful. There was no rigidly controlled experiment and the reactions were chiefly those of the instructor and his students. For what they are worth, they were entirely positive. Another experimental combination brought students together under one instructor for Communication and the introductory philosophy course, Ways of Knowing. Again there was no rigidly controlled experiment, but again the results seemed to be positive and encouraging. It should be noted that these combinations were undertaken on the initiative of individual instructors, who saw possibilities for further reducing the sometimes artificial academic compartments.

Another experimental approach (labelled experimental for administrative reasons) was the institution of an honor section and remedial writing sections. Students were enrolled in the remedial writing sections on the basis of their score on the Cooperative English Test and their work in the first few weeks of the Communication course. Students were enrolled in the honor section during the second semester upon recommendation of their first semester instructor. The honor section covered the same general outline as the other sections but in greater depth. There was, for example, considerably more reading and writing.

A third kind of experimental approach can be noted in the diversity of academic backgrounds of instructors who are chosen to teach in the course. (Only four teachers had previously taught communication.) Whenever possible, "non-English" instructors are encouraged to teach a section of Communication. During the past two years, there have been three such teachers, one in visual communication from the Art Education Division, one in language arts from the Education Department, and one social psychology from the Home Economics Division. Their contributions, especially at bi-weekly staff meetings, were particularly valuable. Of course, the Communication staff has made use of outside lecturers in specific areas from time to time. For example, a television producer, newspaper editor, specialist on film, and specialists in art have lectured to three or four sections during appropriate units of the course.

Some of our experimentation is related to structure and administration. The mechanics of getting large student groups for lectures by experts is facilitated by being able to bring together several sections of the course. Many of the Communication staff teach three sections of the course, and occasionally in the past, one or two members have taught four sections. Whenever this is so, the schedule has been arranged so that all of the sections of one instructor will meet in the auditorium once a week.   This common meeting has allowed the insructor to give lectures or bring in outside lecturers for all of his students at the same time.   It has also made it easy for him to give quizzes and examinations to all of his students at once, to have panel discussions from more than one of his classes, to use films and recordings once instead of three or four times a week.   A further virtue of such an arrangement is that it reduces the number of hours a teacher must spend in a classroom per week.   It should be pointed out that the combined sections are optional for the staff and some teachers have preferred to continue to meet their three sections separately for each meeting of the week.

Another kind of experimental approach involving the staff is the use of an intern-instructor each semester.   By arrangement with the Department of the Teaching of English and Foreign Languages at Teachers College, Columbia University, an advanced graduate student is sent to our campus each semester to take a full teaching load in Communication and one other General Studies Division course, either literature or philosophy.   This intern-instructor is selected by the staff at Teachers College and interviewed by members of the staff at Buffalo State.   Generally speaking, it is a person who has had no college teaching experience, who is well on his way toward his doctorate, is anxious to learn all of the functions of a faculty member, and is ready to try his wings as a teacher (at full pay).   The arrangement began in 1957 and has been particularly successful thus far.   Each instructor has had his own special interest in Communication to bring to both the course and the staff meetings.   Each has been especially conscientious, and each has reported his enthusiastic endorsement of the intern program upon leaving.   The special virtue of the arrangement is that it provides a genuine opportunity for potential college teachers to find out what college teaching is like, to experiment without fear of making mistakes which might be a detriment to their future career at the same institution, and to season their appreciation of graduate courses with some down-to-earth classroom experiences.   The instructors generally return to Teachers College graduate work at the completion of their semester at Buffalo State.

A final list of experimental approaches may be mentioned briefly: about half the instructors of the course band together to produce a single final examination for their sections, and such a group approach is still labelled experimental because many of the faculty feel there are dangers in such an approach; while the staff has agreed to use one basic text for both semesters, each instructor is free to choose his own "reader" for each semester, and this means there is a wide variety of material used and hence a considerable amount of discussion of the virtues of this and that at the bi-weekly staff meetings; a few instructors have experimented with a direct approach to the teaching of listening and have found such an approach valuable and effective for their students.

The Picture in 1970

Any attempt to picture what a Communication course is likely to be in the future is always subject to the hopes and wishes of the writer; hence it is largely subjective and may almost be classified as wishful thinking. Nevertheless, one would hope that the Communication course at this college should concern itself more directly with communication in the campus community. Students would begin to think of communication not simply as reading, writing, and speaking but as a vital factor in the effectiveness of the total community. One would hope that such an attitude would be reflected in assignments of more far-reaching implications than the sometimes sterile assignments of the present time. Of course one would also hope that all classes, not simply those labelled "Communication," would have a greater concern for more effective expression.

Within the course itself one would hope that the majority of the members of the staff would have as their chief concern effective teaching of Communication. Such a staff would be more concerned with having students observe good language usage rather than learning the rules of grammar. Such a staff might well include three or four specialists in each of the mass media. Such a staff would be interested in bringing to this campus visiting lecturers of national repute in several of the areas of the Communication course, perhaps arranging summer workshops and graduate courses for such lecturers. Such a staff would also offer genuine encouragement to a variety of creative projects, ranging perhaps from designing model communities to writing poems and short stories. A foretaste of such projects is evident in a heightened interest in the course by members of our nationally prominent art education division. These "artists" view communication as an integral part of their "province," and they want to explore ways of working with the communication staff.

What one would wish for the future and what is possible for the future are not always the same thing, but wishing is the first step in the process of making the possible, and with continued support from the faculty and administration, we may continue to chip away at the design of a truly effective course in communication.

chapter 18

THE USES OF LANGUAGE AT RENSSELAER POLYTECHNIC INSTITUTE

Sterling P. Olmsted* and Wentworth K. Brown**

The Present Course

This experimental course originated in the belief that "freshman English" can contribute more to general college education than is usually expected of it. Where the students are well prepared and where the English staff is able and genuinely interested in teaching, freshman English should aspire to something more adult and more original than a rehash of composition problems or an extension of the same kind of literary study now initiated pretty effectively by the high schools.

Accordingly, The Uses of Language is designed to make several positive contributions, simultaneously and quite deliberately, to a college-level education. However, the course's most original contributions derive from its focus, which is on language. The study centers on language — what it is all about, how it works in its chief uses. The overriding object is to get students to think, and think hard, about language, viewed as a means not only of communicating and expressing but also of seeing and thinking. Language is both end and means in the course, subject matter and method. Within this framework, the course aims to be at

---

*Head, Department of Language and Literature.
**Professor of English.

[1] (The course is English 9.11 at Rensselaer Polytechnic Institute. It is worth three credit hours, occupies one of eight semesters of a 24-hour, Institute-wide general studies program. is required for all freshmen in either the first or second term, and has been offered continuously since 1953-4.)

least four things at once: an adult introduction to language itself;
a "types of literature" course of a special sort; an insight via
language, into certain basic philosophical problems germane to the
study of language; and a fresh means of improving reading and
writing.

1. *Study of Language*

A systematic inquiry into three main uses of language gives
the course both its intellectual discipline and its structure. The
course begins by introducing language, as the most crucial and
universal of all the symbolisms man has devised for handling
his experience. This point of view proves novel to college students
to whom language has previously meant little more than dictionaries full of words and handbooks full of rules.

The course then continues in three main units, each concerned
with one of the principal uses of language. The reduction of the
uses to three is a simplifying device, useful pedagogically. The
three are defined as the "informative" use (language intended primarily to convey abstract or intellectual knowledge), the "creative"
use (language intended to create experience), and the "persuasive"
use (language intended to influence attitudes and — ultimately —
actions). These three uses are shown to account for most of man's
formal, public word-using. The student is not led to believe,
however, that this classification is either complete or ultimate. And
as he examines these uses, the student himself recognizes the less
common ones, the more private ones, and many combinations of
uses.

The method of the course is essentially comparative, the three
main uses being studied in relation to one another and with references to nonverbal media (e.g., mathematics, graphics, the visual
arts, and music). To facilitate comparison, certain basic questions
are raised about each main use:

a. How do words work in language used for this purpose?

b. According to what principles is language organized
in this use?

c. What kinds of "statement" are found in this use?

d. What are the "values" of this use of language?

e. What criteria are appropriate in judging writing which
embodies this use?

In dealing with these questions, the course draws on several disciplines, notably anthropology, epistemology, aesthetics, literary criticism, psychology, and propaganda analysis.

In spite of this reliance on established bodies of theory, however, the technique of the course is essentially inductive. Students use a "theory" text, prepared by members of the staff, less to "get the real scoop" than to grasp the questions more readily. Students also work with selected writings which embody the three main uses of language in relatively pure forms and in various combinations and mixtures. Since the primary subject is language rather than literature, these specimens include ephemeral stuff (from current newspapers and magazines) as well as anthologized material. On all key questions of theory, students are encouraged to work toward solutions on their own before being offered any answers *ex-cathedra*, either by the instructor or in the text.

2. Study of literature by "types"

Any study of language of the sort just described is bound to be also a study of literature. Thus the concept of uses gives us a classification of literature according to purpose (informative, creative, and persuasive). And this way of classifying has several advantages, pedagogically, over the more usual division (Non-fiction, Fiction, Poetry, and Drama, each with its subtypes.)

1. Literature is seen to be an intimate part of man's total activity. The all-important questions of purpose and value, therefore, are constantly in the foreground of the student's mind as he reads and discusses what he has read.

2. The concept of literature itself naturally broadens to include not only anthology but also everyday material. This widening of the province of literature invites comparisons of good and bad writing.

3. Comparisons between literature and works in the nonverbal media are facilitated because all media, verbal and nonverbal alike, are seen as serving the same basic human needs and purposes.

4. New similarities among and divisions within the traditional literary forms become apparent. For example, the writings of news reporters, encyclopedists, historians, scientists, and most philosophers are seen to share one basic purpose ("informative"). In like manner, the poet, dramatist, and fiction writers are

obviously engaged in the same basic job: the creation of experience. And the student learns to spot persuasive purpose in any of these forms, and to separate it from the primary purpose of such writings.

5. When studied in close juxtaposition to informative and persuasive literature, creative writing tends to be recognized for what it really is — an art form, closer in all important respects to nonverbal works of art than to other literature.

6. When the three uses of language (or kinds of literature) are studied comparatively, certain general principles (of word-use, organization, value, etc.) tend to stand out — principles which often are lost in a mass of technical details.

To sum up: dividing literature into informative, creative, and persuasive enables us to come closer to the heart of many literary problems. This grouping is a little like the geologist's classification of rocks into igneous, sedimentary, and metamorphic: both sets of categories are particularly useful because they are based on *origin*. By contrast, the standard classification used in most "types of literature" courses is like proposing to study rocks by examining a few (carefully polished) specimens of — say — marble, granite. slate, and opal.

Despite these several ways in which The Uses of Language contributes to the student's understanding of literature, the course is not primarily an introduction to literature. The focal subject is language; and literature is simply language going about its various jobs in formal dress.

3. *An introduction to some philosophical problems*

Neither was the course designed to serve as an introduction to philosophy, and it makes no pretense at replacing any orthodox course in philosophy. It acquired a philosophical dimension quite naturally, however, as a direct outgrowth of its emphasis on language.

The approach to language and literature described above requires at least an explanatory consideration of several philosophical problems. Most obviously, the problem of symbols and how they "mean" is central to any discussion of language; thus some attention to semantics is essential. Likewise, the problems of epistemology must at least be raised in any thoughtful discussion of the "informative" use of language. The question of the nature of knowledge becomes particularly important when, as in this course, the informative use is taken to mean not only the communicating of facts but also the use of words as the medium for conceptualizing and "knowing" in the intellectual sense. Similarly, our investigation into the "creative" use of language involves the student in some of the central issues of aesthetics. And the discussion of "persuasive" language introduces problems which belong properly to ethics and even to politics.

No attempt is made, of course, to pursue any of these questions very far. But the problems are posed, the students are made aware of them, and sometimes tentative answers are suggested. It should be added, perhaps, that these introductory excursions into philosophy are not forced marches. They occur quite naturally in the process of arriving at an understanding of language, and they are pursued only as far as they are useful to this purpose.

4. An approach to reading and writing

It may appear that The Uses of Language in its various objectives has inverted the usual order of precedence: the development of skills is listed in fourth place, after language, literature, and philosophy. Actually, a major objective of the course has always been to advance the student's ability to handle language both as reader and as writer: the approach is simply more indirect than that taken in pre-college English programs or in many freshman "skill" courses.

The theoretical study of language gives students a new orientation toward the whole business of writing and reading. They become aware of the varying purposes of writers, and they learn to "shift gears" as they move from one use of language to another. This is part of what one staff member meant when he called this "a course in how to read The New Yorker." The course furnishes a conceptual framework within which readers more readily grasp the rationale of unfamiliar kinds of reading.

Besides giving him this more adequate frame of reference, the course also offers several practical rules, derived directly from the theory of language. For example, the principle of plurisignation (multiple meaning) is shown to be fundamental to the operation of creative language; this means that in dealing with imaginative literature one must expect words (and larger units as well) to mean differently (in several ways at once) than is usual in informative writing. Or, again, the principle of similarity-and-difference (parallelism-and-contrast) is shown to apply generally to the structure of creative literature, as it does to all artistic structure; from this the student sees that to perceive the form of a difficult poem or a subtle short story one must watch for parallels and contrasts, repetitions and variations on them, conflicts and tensions. Or, again, having seen how fundamentally unlike informative and persuasive writing poems and plays are, he stops looking for the stanza with "the moral" or the scene that states the great philosophical truth.

Third, in developing theory inductively, the course at the same time provides practice in careful, thoughtful, critical reading. No perfunctory skimming will do. The student learns to note purpose, form, and the detailed handling of words, and he also begins to discriminate between the excellent, mediocre, and inferior.

How much time is left over for writing? Not much. But nearly all the work of the course is related to writing. The student writes a good deal — not as an extra, however. All of this writing is functional to the course: it employs language in the study of language. And most of this writing is annotated and criticized by the instructor, not merely for handbook correctness (though handbook symbols are used) but also in the light of the subject-matter of the course.

While he is practicing writing as part of the necessary work of the course, the student is also sharpening his own perceptions. As he learns *about* language, he also progresses in his own *use of* language as a means of communicating, expressing, thinking, and becoming aware. Most important, he tends to become more critical of his own thinking and ways of expressing himself and more conscious of the intimate relationship between these two.

Changes Now in Progress

Methods and materials have changed gradually from year to year. Even the objectives have shifted (or perhaps they have simply become clearer). For example, the conception outlined here is more complex and less mechanical than was our original notion of the course.

The germinal idea of three basic uses of language has not changed. But whereas we once thought of this division as simply a framework within which to study three kinds of writing (primarily to develop more sophisticated readers), we now suspect that involved in this idea is the whole business of the differing but complementary ways in which man registers, interprets, and communicates his experience.

One major problem has beset the course from the beginning: there is no unified "field theory" of language which takes into account all three uses. Theorists of language have limited their attention pretty exclusively to either the informative or the creative uses, and none has given any serious philosophical attention to the third use, the "persuasive." The biggest piece of unfinished business in the course is the development of a coherent theory. So far, we have used a mosaic of ideas and principles, some of which are inimical to one another. For example, it is becoming increasingly clear that some of the basic definitions of popular semantics (developed largely by thinkers of the positivist persuasion) are prejudicial to all respectable theories of literary art. The most important current developments in the course are in theory-making. This year, text material is being supplemented with lectures in an attempt to present theories more clearly and consistently. And text materials are being revised.

The Course in 1970

If we can solve the problem of theory, the course ten years from now will be not only more coherent conceptually, but more centered on the particular needs of the individual student If language is thought of as an instrument for communicating, creating, conceptualizing, and experiencing, then this course, since it centers on language, will be more and more concerned with the way the individual student uses and may use language to do these things. But an increasing emphasis on the experience and needs of the student presupposes the further development of the concepts behind the course. It is now apparent to some of us that the idea of language as an instrument either for transferring information about the objective world, or for manipulating other people, or even for creating experience is inadequate. Much of man's utterance is an attempt to reassure himself that his subjective experiences are shared by others. Many of his "informative statements" are essentially hypotheses. The man who makes them wants and expects to have them checked by others. In this view, language assumes an even

greater importance than we tend to assign to it today.   In all its
forms it is a means whereby the individual escapes from his own
subjectivity, sharing experience with others or establishing a common body of concepts.

    This emphasis on the individual's subjective experience will
not only provide a more coherent and sophisticated body of theory
(although more difficult); it will also compel us to pay greater
attention to the individual student's experience and his handling
of language.   What all this will mean in the structure and content
of the course is not yet clear.   But we think it will become even
less deductive and more inductive, more coherent and at the same
time more flexible.

chapter 19

THE COMMUNICATION PROGRAM AT ST. CLOUD STATE COLLEGE

*T. A. Barnhart, Charles Baleer, and William Donnelly**

We can't go as far as Humpty Dumpty in saying: "When I use a word, it means just what I choose it to mean, neither more nor less." But just as obviously, we can't go to the other extreme and say that when we use "communication" it means neither more nor less than the dictionary says it does. If that were true, there would be no reason for this book. So to make clear what we mean, we had better begin by defining the term as we use it.

By "communication" we at St. Cloud State College mean the fundamental processes of observing and reporting activities in all areas of life, of making inferences and expressing them suitably, and of evaluating the reports and opinions of others. By communication we mean oral as well as written activity, non-verbal as well as verbal, and most of all, we mean a process that must be understood in all of its interrelated phases: the communicator, the message, the receiver, the medium, the purpose, and the context.

This definition fits naturally into the larger framework of the college statement of philosophy, reprinted in each new edition of the catalogue. The statement says in part:

> Education, if it is to be effective, must provide for every member of its society capable of receiving it a respectable body of accumulated knowledge and the skills and opportunities for using it to his profit and to the ad-

---

*T. A. Barnhart is Chairman of the Division of Languages and Literature, Charles Baleer is Director of Communication, William Donnelly is in charge of Communication 233 and Communication 234.

vantages of many; it must create situations favorable to the development of discriminating judgment; it must encourage self-development and self-realization; it must furnish the impulse toward wider understanding and sympathy; it must instill an attitude of personal responsibility.[1]

It is the assumption of the communication staff at St. Cloud State College that the development of awareness and skill in the fundamental processes of communication is basic to the pursuit of all of these educational goals.

In addition to the underlying philosophy one of the basic factors in shaping the content and organization of a communication program must inevitably be the level of communication effectiveness already attained by the students themselves. For a variety of reasons the level of communication awareness and skill of a typical entering freshman at St. Cloud is relatively low. Many students come from small towns or farms where the emphasis has been on activities of a practical or physical orientation rather than a cultural or intellectual one. In addition the legislative policy that the state colleges be open to all high school graduates makes it inevitable that the high school performance record of the average entering freshman is somewhat lower than it would be for colleges with selective standards. As a result a substantial number of entering students tend to be fairly unsophisticated in their use of language and somewhat superficial in their knowledge of and attitude toward the various communication media. On the other hand, many of these students show considerable responsiveness to new ideas in communication, as if a whole undeveloped area of potential ability were being tapped.

The communication sequence is clearly a part of the General Education program with its primary emphasis on individual self fulfillment. But there is a particular need at St. Cloud State College for developing skill in communication and an understanding of the intricate relationships involved in the communication process. The reason is that 71 per cent of the students at the college are preparing to be teachers, and will soon be adding to their own communication responsibilities the responsibility of developing

---

[1] *1959-1961 Catalogue*, St. Cloud State College, p. 100.

communication skills and a communication philosophy in their students.

The communication sequence consists of three basic courses — Communication 131, 132, and 233 — but there are variations. Students who receive a mark of either "D" or "E" in any course must repeat it before proceeding to the next course in the sequence. In addition, some Communication 131 students are given an "X" grade, and they must take a special two-credit course, Communication 031, before going on to Communication 132. Special tutoring sections taught by graduate students and paid for by participating students are set up on a voluntary basis. For students whose achievement in English 131 indicates ability to profit by an enriched program, English 142 is offered in place of English 132 and English 243 is offered in place of English 233.

Communication 131

Communication 131, meeting four times a week for four credits, is the first of a sequence of three courses in communication required of all students at St. Cloud State College. During the 1958-59 school year 44 sections of Communication 131 were offered with an average enrollment of 26 students.

Communication 131 tries to help the student: to evaluate his needs and abilities in communication; to develop more mature skills in reading, writing, speaking and listening; and to understand the value of effective communication to himself and to his society. To accomplish these aims, purposeful communication is stressed, and the skills are taught in an integrated manner. Therefore, the similarities and differences are noted between the presentation skills of speaking and writing and the receptive skills of reading and listening. Both expository and persuasive speaking and writing are studied. Subjects for five-minute talks and individual paragraphs or short compositions are selected from ideas explored in a book of readings and related to the student's own experience. When a student speaks or writes, he is expected to have an idea that he feels is worthwhile and to adapt his subject and method of presentation to his purpose and to the needs of his audience. Usually sentence outlines, consisting of an introduction, controlling idea, body, and conclusion, are prepared beforehand.

Mechanics of expression are taught whenever the need occurs, but students are urged to assume the responsibility for observing certain minimum essentials in all their written work.

When students read or listen to fellow-students, they are expected to note controlling ideas and main divisions of thought. To aid them in reading and listening critically, some attention is given to these aspects of thinking: inductive and deductive reasoning, distinguishing between facts and opinions, and recognizing the relationships between ideas. Variety and concreteness in developing ideas are also illustrated in the readings and practiced in writing and speaking. Thus, Communication 131 not only tries to help the student present his own ideas in a clear, believable, and interesting manner; but it also tries to help him understand and evaluate the ideas of others.

Evaluation includes utilizing the STEP Writing Test scores. Form A is given during freshman testing week and Form B is given the last week of the quarter. A "green paper" is also written by each student during a two-hour period set aside at the end of the quarter, and this is evaluated by a team of staff members other than the student's regular instructor. Emphasis of this evaluation is on organization, development, and logic, as well as mechanics of expression. The individual instructor evaluates the students during the quarter by the use of a "minimum essentials check list," weekly paragraphs or themes, and three or four expository speeches. Extensive use is made by instructors of the opaque projector for class discussion and evaluation of paragraphs and themes, as well as mimeographed copies of student writing for class comment. The N.C.T.E. Ideaform paper is used for all written work.

The texts are: *Effective Communication* by Wayne Thompson and *Ideas in Process* edited by C. Merton Babcock. *Effective Communication* presents basic information about the four skills and provides a handbook for writing. *Ideas in Process*, on the other hand, is a collection of largely expository writings from contemporary magazines like *Harper's, Fortune,* and *The American Scholar.* These selections stimulate thinking and illustrate various aspects of the communication process like selecting ideas, deciding on purpose, or distinguishing fact from opinion.

Communication 031

Communication 031, meeting two times a week for one quarter for two credits, is required of students whose performance in

Communication 131 indicates deficiencies in oral or written communication not sufficiently serious to warrant a mark of "D" or "E." Successful completion—a grade of "C" or better—results in a "C" mark in Communication 131 and enables the student to enter Communication 132. Failure in Communication 031 requires the student to repeat Communication 131. Last year, 1958-59, approximately 165 were recommended for Communication 031 out of a freshman class of 800. In contrast, 160 students received grades of "D" or "E." Approximately 415 students were admitted to Communication 132 and 60 recommended for the enriched course, Communication 142.

The aim of Communication 031 is remediation in those areas of writing and/or speaking which are causing the student difficulties in his communication. Experience indicates that most of the trouble centers around mechanics of expression and usage. Approximately 62 per cent of those registered for Communication 031 during 1958-59 passed and became eligible for Communication 132.

The text for this course has been Suberman and Rosenberg's _Basic Composition_. No specific speech text has been used.

The other aspect of the St. Cloud remedial program is the recommendation to special tutoring sections for students whose performance and entrance test scores indicate serious problems in writing. These sections, limited to six students each, are taught by graduate students or qualified seniors majoring in language arts. Each student pays for this help himself, and the only college control is that the director of Communication organizes, supervises, and arranges for time and place of meeting of the tutoring groups.

Communication 132

Communication 132, four credits, is the second course in the regular communication sequence. During 1958-59, 34 sections were offered with an average enrollment of 26 students.

The general goal of Communication 132, as of Communication 131, is the development of skills of listening, reading, writing, and speaking commensurate with college work. However, Communication 132 is oriented toward techniques involved in research writing and problem-solving discussion. While the course of study includes assigned expository readings, class discussion, led by class members, individual speeches, panel discussions, and research papers receive the main emphasis.

The basic texts currently used are a book of readings, *Writer's Resource Book* by John Gerber and Kenneth Houp; a handbook on oral and written communication, *Fundamentals of Communication* by Wayne Thompson; and *The Research Manual* by Cecil B. Williams and Alan H. Stevenson. Each student is expected to own a college-level dictionary and Thomas C. Pollock's *Spelling Report*.

Each student participates in approximately six class discussions on the ideas contained in the readings in Gerber and Houp. Using a discussion outline, the students are expected to conduct themselves with a minimum of teacher direction. These class discussions of assigned readings serve to develop and to evaluate student skills in reading, speaking, and listening.

Each member of a class participates in two formal discussions of the panel and/or symposium type. Topics are selected by the students from problems of importance and interest growing out of the readings and class discussions. Individual preparation for the panels includes making a bibliography, reading library sources, and writing documented note cards. (All students have already had specific library orientation sessions given by members of the library staff during freshman orientation periods.)

Each student writes at least two research papers. The first paper is frequently prepared step by step in class as the techniques for research writing are being taught. The student may select a problem for research from a prepared list representing a variety of areas, or he may choose a topic of special interest to him with the approval of the instructor.

Each student gives two formal speeches. The first comes within the first two weeks of the quarter and is usually persuasive in nature. The second comes at the end of the quarter and is often an oral presentation of the research done for the final research paper.

During the last week of the quarter students are given Form B of the STEP Listening Test. These scores are compared with the Form A scores secured during freshman testing week.

Communication 142

Communication 142 is a course for those students whose achievement in Communication 131 indicates an ability to profit from an advanced and enriched program. Students are recommended by their Communication 131 instructor and admitted on recommendation of the Division. Three sections were offered during 1958-59 with a total of 60 students enrolled out of a freshman class of 800.

The basic structure of this course is the same as Communication 132 with the emphasis on discussion and research. The texts are the same with the exception of the book of readings. In Communication 142, Durling, Sickels and Viljoen's *An Invitation to Thought, Discussion, and Writing* is used. Topics covered in the discussions and used as bases for research writings include: Sciences of Nature and Man; Freedom and the Tests of Democracy; Crises of Race and Relations of Peoples; Intuition and Reason; and Experience and Art.

Communication 233

Communication 233 is the third course in the regular 12-credit communication sequence. Partly for administrative reasons and partly on the hard-to-prove assumption that students with a year of college behind them can put sufficiently more into the course to get significantly more real value from it, the course is offered at the sophomore level. The course continues the emphasis on developing communication skills to fit a wide variety of purposes, but the content of the course is provided by analysis and evaluation of contemporary communication media. Newspapers and magazines, television and moving pictures provide a particularly stimulating body of materials for probing, fact-finding themes or lively, problem-solving discussions. The accent throughout the course is on developing a background of knowledge and factual information about the media, applying critical judgment techniques to specific media performances, and using these to develop general standards of selection, appreciation, and evaluation.

The course begins with a four-week unit on semantics, logic, propaganda analysis, and general critical thinking skills. Students are introduced to the unit by viewing selected kinescopes from *Talking Sense,* an outstanding educational television series on semantics by the late Irving J. Lee. The text for the unit is *Preface to Critical Reading* by Richard D. Altick. Two additional films, *Production 5118* and *Communications Primer,* are also shown during the first few weeks.

The remaining seven weeks of the course are used for a short, intensive unit on magazines, a short, intensive unit on newspapers, and a series of research panels on books, moving pictures, radio and television, and problems of freedom and censorship. A considerable portion of class time is used for small group planning meetings for each of these activities. There are at least two half-period planning sessions for group reports on newspapers, at least two for magazines, and three for the research panels.

For the magazine reports the class is divided into five panels with each panel taking responsibility for a different group of magazines. (With some straining to fit each magazine into a specific category, the magazines are classified arbitrarily into the slicks, the quality group, the news magazines, the special interest group, and the idea magazines. Each teacher uses a special roundup period to discuss magazines like the pulps which don't fit into these categories.) Making liberal use of specific illustrative materials from the magazines themselves, each panel takes one class period to present the significant points of similarity and difference of the magazines in its group. In addition each student writes an 800 to 1000 word theme analyzing and evaluating the editorial formula of one particular magazine from his group.

For the newspaper reports ten morning newspapers and ten evening papers are ordered from various parts of the country on the same day. Oral reports are divided into five informal panels with one period for each: news presentation in the ten morning papers; editorial pages in the ten morning papers; news presentation in ten evening papers; editorial pages in ten evening papers; and special features (sports, comics, business, women's pages, etc.) in ten selected papers. For a written report each student prepares a simple statistical analysis and writes an 800 word report on one pair of papers in his particular category (news, editorials, or special features). The focus for all reports is on bringing out significant points of similarity or difference in the papers, basing all opinions on specific examples of good or bad features, and always keeping in mind an awareness that judgments are being made tentatively within the framework of one day's performance.

Each student participates in one of four research panels (about six or seven to a panel) and each panel takes two class periods to present its material. The panels are instructed to use an informal, problem-solving approach with much give and take of free discussion, but considerable stress is placed on the importance of a thorough foundation of background reading. Each student is expected to quote frequently from his reading with the quoted material providing a stimulus for discussion and supporting evidence for personal opinion. Students are expected to submit a full set of note cards and bibliography cards (at least 20 sources) one week before the panel so that the teacher can evaluate them, become familiar with the material, and subsequently judge the extent to which each student is making creative use of his research during the panels. Students are given a list of possible key questions from which they can select several to use as the springboard for their discussion. As with all other activities of the course, the purpose of the panels is two-fold: to provide a means for stimulating the thinking of all students in the class about the functions, potentialities and limitations of the various communication media, and to provide a thoroughly motivated exercise in good discussion technique based on a solid foundation of advance preparation.

In addition to these activities there is one other out-of-class theme, a movie review based on a selected list of five movies shown locally during the quarter. Along with the student's personal evaluation of the picture, he is expected to compare his judgments with the reviews of at least three professional critics. The course also includes an in-class theme (written during a two-hour period in test week) in which each student applies the critical thinking techniques he has learned to an analysis and evaluation of a particularly loaded magazine advertisement.

Communication 243

Communication 243, the enriched course taken by superior students in lieu of Communication 233, makes use of many of the activities that have proved successful in the basic course: the intensive study of newspapers and magazines, the research panels on the various media and on censorship. However, the unit on semantics and critical thinking skills is shortened from four weeks to approximately one week of class time with more reading in this area done by the students outside of class. The time saved is used for activities in cross media analysis; comparisons of the techniques used by the various media in telling a story, in reporting an event, in disseminating information, in achieving aesthetic effects, or in trying to make people laugh. The particular potentialities and limitations of each medium are analyzed and evaluated. These activities have been experimental but it is highly likely that those which have proved most successful will be adapted to the program of Communication 233.

The text used for Communication 243 is *Our Language and Our World*, edited by S. I. Hayakawa. The book is composed of articles from *ETC.* (1953-58) which apply semantics principles to communication in public affairs, education, both the highbrow and lowbrow arts, and human relations generally. The articles provide a stimulating background for the students in their own subsequent application of semantics principles to the analysis of communication media.

Staff

Staff members who teach the communication courses are all members of the Division of Languages and Literature. The only faculty of this division not used for these general education courses are members teaching full time in foreign languages or speech correction. It is felt that part of the strength of the program is the diversity of staff background and training. Individuals with major training in literature, writing, speech, language arts — all combine to teach the basic communication sequence. Weekly staff meetings during a two-hour Monday lunch period provide valuable in-service training. Although the normal teaching load at St. Cloud is 16 quarter hours, faculty teaching full-time communication courses teach only 12 quarter hours.

For the past two years graduate assistants (students working on their M.S. degree in Education with a major in English or Speech) have been hired on a part-time basis to help staff the Communications 131 and 031 courses. To date this has proved very satisfactory. These assistants are supervised by the Director of Communication, given a detailed syllabus of the course for aid, and they enroll as part of their graduate program in the fall quarter of their first teaching year in a special course in Language Arts (Communication) Problems.

This past year, in an effort to make the entire college community conscious of the importance of communication — both faculty and students — we solicited the aid of other faculty members by asking them to refuse to read poorly-written papers. Gummed labels were provided and instructors were asked to hand the paper back with the attached label indicating that until the English in the paper was improved the paper would not be read for content. Almost the entire faculty, 95%, requested stickers.

Problems for the Future

Since 1956, enrollment at St. Cloud has consistently exceeded the long-term predictions. For instance, in 1956 it was estimated that 2,200 students would enroll in the fall quarter of 1958. Actually 2,600 enrolled. It was estimated in 1956 that 2,300 would enroll in 1959. Preregistration up to August, 1959, forecasts a freshman and transfer enrollment of not less than 1,200 and a total enrollment of 3,000. This is an increase of more than 150 per cent over the 1952 enrollment of less than 1,200.

The Communication Program is prepared to offer 34-40 sections of English 131, with 30 students to the section, during the fall and winter quarters of 1959-60. The 7-8 sections scheduled for spring are intended primarily for students entering that quarter and for those who have failed the course in the first two quarters. It is possible that for a year or two of continual increases, sufficient staff can be found to staff the program at the present class maximums (already higher than the limits per class set a few years ago). But the strain will increase constantly in two areas: the state's ability and willingness to tax itself to support such staff increases, and the department's resourcefulness in securing the additional necessary staff when recent reports from the graduate schools are anything but reassuring.

The department wishes to continue the individualized and diversified program it now has, making the modifications and improvements that inevitably suggest themselves in staff evaluation sessions. But enrollment pressures and the resultant problem of finding and paying for the additional staff needed may force a choice between eliminating some aspects of the present program or of searching out ways to do the same work with as great efficiency but with less effort. The department intends, if it is possible, to continue to include such important matters as research, semantics, linguistics, evaluation of the mass media, and other specialized studies now commonly a part of most communication programs. But such specialization will continue to require an unusually favorable student-teacher ratio. Lectures and other methods of mass language instruction are scarcely acceptable substitutes for hard and continuous experience in using language under the guidance of capable and experienced instructors.

If the department continues its present methods of instruction (and recent experimentation throughout the country does not seem to offer any adequate substitute), it is likely there will be no choice between increasing the size of the staff and increasing the size of classes. Both will be unavoidable. It will therefore be necessary to employ as instructors more people with the Master's degree who have permanently or temporarily given up plans for advanced degrees; perhaps to double the number of transient staff by recruiting more part time assistants from the graduate program of the Speech and English departments; and to shift to the shoulders of those students who are unable to make satisfactory progress the financial burden of tutorial help, formal or informal.

Any marked change in requirements in the courses must be preceded by conference between the high school and the college instructors to determine just what the latter have a right to require of freshman students and what the former believe they can reasonably be expected to offer and require of the high school student. The department at St. Cloud plans to continue and expand its meetings with high school teachers and to produce and publish within two years a mutually agreed upon set of minimum essentials for the college freshman writer.

Should the shortage of prepared instructors become as acute as some fear that it will, it may be necessary to reserve the time of the staff to a much greater extent than is customary now for actual instruction. This could be accomplished in part by developing an organized plan of mutual help and criticism among the students themselves. Or it could go further than that to a modification of a plan now being tried out experimentally in selected high schools: the recruitment of a "married women" corps from the community to handle the major burden of theme correction and possibly some of the clerical details of class management as well.

chapter 20

THE COMMUNICATION SKILLS PROGRAM AT THE UNITED STATES AIR FORCE AIR UNIVERSITY

*Joseph H. Mahaffey**

Air University

Air University, one of the major commands of the United States Air Force, was established in 1946 to provide a unified and integrated educational program for career officers. It is the graduate school of the Air Force and should not be confused with the Air Force Academy, the undergraduate school at Colorado Springs, Colorado. Air University is a unique military command where, in the words of General Carl Spaatz, officers are given the opportunity "to think into the future . . . to see the world . . . as it will be in five years' time or a decade." Formally stated, its mission is to prepare officers for command of squadrons, groups, wings, and larger Air Force units and for staff duties with all types of Air Force organizations. In addition, Air University provides education to meet the scientific and technical requirements of the Air Force; it administers the widely dispersed Air Force ROTC program in 191 civilian colleges and universities; and it conducts the Extension Course Institute, a correspondence system of home study for active duty, reserve, and civilian personnel.

The hard core of our professional education program is made up of three schools — Squadron Officer School, Command and

---

*Consultant in Communication Skills, Academic Instructor School, Air University, Maxwell Air Force Base, Alabama.

Staff College, and War College. All three schools are intended to prepare officers for command and staff duties of increasing complexity. Therefore the curriculums differ not so much in the things that are done as in the complexity of the things that are done. A highly capable officer, for example, should expect to attend the Squadron Officer School after five years of service, the Command and Staff College at the ten-year service level, and the War College at about the 15-year level of service. However, Air University concentrates its efforts on quality rather than quantity. Each progressive level of schooling represents a rigid "screening" process. Officers who attend the command and Staff College and the War College are selected by boards of senior officers in Headquarters, United States Air Force, in much the same manner as they would be chosen for promotion to higher rank. Under present conditions less than 15 percent of eligible officers can expect to attend either of these two schools.

I have emphasized the three general service schools, not only because they constitute the base of our professional education program, but also because they are among the schools that the Communication Techniques Division is especially designed to service. My purpose in this article is to present a brief rationale for communication skills instruction in certain air University schools and to outline more specifically the procedures used in our teaching.

I

I am employed as an educational specialist in communication skills and am assigned to the Academic Instructor School, of which the Communication Techniques Division is a part. The best way I can make our organizational function clear is to compare it with that of an English or Speech Department in a civilian college. If the college administration were to abolish this department as such and attach its members to the President's staff as experts in communication on the theory that communication permeated all that he did as a supervisor, then the position of those members in that school would be somewhat analogous to the position we hold in the schools of Air University. If this college president were to say to his communication specialists, study everything that is done in this college, select every opportunity to teach communication instruction in every department, work directly with the faculty on planning methods for using communication in their respective subjects, train my teachers to use and criticize communication, and help me supervise all manifestations of communication, then they and we would have basically the same functions.

The Communication Techniques Division, composed of seven officers, is charged with the mission of planning and presenting programs of instruction in communicative skills for four Air University schools — Squadron Officer School, Command and Staff College, Academic Instructor School, and the Allied Officer Preparatory Course — and, upon request, to the War College and to other components of the University. These programs include faculty and student education incident to learning and successfully using problem solving techniques, logical and creative thinking, semantics, oral and written expression, professional reading and reading improvement, listening, group discussion and group dynamics, negotiation, human relations, and audio-visual communication. The division provides overall professional advice and keeps Air University informed of the latest research in the field of communication.

In our teaching we operate on the assumption that the acquisition of these skills leads to a better understanding and use of professional military knowledge. Certainly, Air Force officers face exceedingly complicated national and international problems upon which they are expected to make a judgment. To understand these issues, our officers must be able to think logically and read, listen, speak, and write effectively. What an individual feels, thinks, and knows has no significance unless he can transmit meaning from himself to others. In short, he establishes and maintains relationships with the world in which he lives through communication.

From this point of view, then, communication skills are the basic tools of commanders and staff officers, irrespective of their assignment or specialty within the Air Force. Unless the officer has learned to use well the communicative devices available to him so that he can get his message understood by others, and so that he can understand others, he will fail to integrate the activities of his subordinates or to gain the support of those outside his appointed leadership. Particularly is this true as he moves up the ladder of command into those positions for which Air University is especially designed to prepare him. The higher the level of supervision, the greater the need for skill in communicating with all other levels.

Our approach to communication skills instruction is largely determined by the command and staff frame of reference. Our work must support the overall mission of each school or college. Except for a few special laboratories, planned communicative experiences are never exercises for the sake of drill alone. This concept is essential, not only to save curriculum time, but also for ease of transfer of learning to field situations. For example, not every type of writing is taught, but only writing typically required in command and staff positions. A commander brings an entirely different orientation to the problem of writing a directive or a staff study report than an essayist brings to essay or a poet to a poem. Group discussion is taught in relation to staff conferences and multiple management; human relations to the need of the officer to work with others; listening techniques to the commander's use of interviewing, counseling, and conferring. In all instruction we want the student to visualize himself as a member of a command-staff team. It is this insistence on the command-staff perspective that imparts to our instruction in communication skills a different character from that usually found in the civilian college or university.

Regardless of his degree of proficiency, no student is exempted from our program. Since communication is always conducted as a social activity, and since social patterns are infinitely complex, we do not recognize a point of absolute mastery of any one of the communication skills. No man is ever a perfect speaker; no man a perfect writer. We believe that all officers can profit from instruction and from criticism of their performance.

The kind of instructional methods used, the extent of coverage given to each skill, and the intensity of treatment varies with several factors. Among these factors are: (1) the experience or maturity level of the students, (2) the complexity of the command and staff activities being treated in the particular school, (3) the length of the school, and (4) the pressure of other substantive material needed to accomplish the mission of the school. We give special attention to the differences in requirements at different levels in the Air Force organizational structure. For the lieutenants and captains in the Squadron Officer School, we emphasize communicative techniques needed in small organizations where the commander and staff are close to the problems and people involved in the actual operations. For the senior captains and majors in the Command and Staff College, we stress those techniques required in complex organizations where commanders and staff officers must work primarily through intermediaries to reach those handling the details of actual operation. By emphasizing the requirements of different organizational levels for such skills and by making variations in emphasis and methods of instruction, we seek to insure the highest degree of personal competence in all officers at all echelons.

II

For the sake of clarity, let us take a closer look at one Air University school — the Command and Staff College — and its communicative skills program.

The Command and Staff College is of nine and one-half months duration. The student body is composed of approximately 600 selected officers who hold the rank of major or captain. This college provides the intermediate level of professional education within the Air University system. Officers attending it have had schooling or experience in squadron duties and usually experience on wing or higher staffs. In general, they have reached a transitional point in their careers when they need broader knowledge and ability to solve the increasingly complex problems of future aerospace power employment. For a great proportion of these officers, the Command and Staff College terminates their formal military education.

The general objectives of Unit I, "Individual Skills," are that the student improve his ability to:

1. Communicate precisely and clearly in terms appropriate to the intended audience.
2. Comprehend, analyze, and interpret the communications of others.
3. Use a logical and systematic method in solving military problems.
4. Use committee action as an aid in accomplishing military tasks.

Communication skills instruction is heavily stressed at the outset to give the student the opportunity to practice these skills throughout the school year. He attains the desired learning outcomes of

subsequent units in the curriculum in direct proportion to his
ability to synthesize and apply the skills taught in Unit I.

Perhaps I should mention at this point the emphasis upon
small group work in our educational program. Each student spends
about half of each school day in a 14-man seminar group under
the immediate supervision of a faculty adviser. The basic purpose
of the seminar is to reinforce the learning acquired from previous
lectures, required readings, and other seminars. Some seminars
simply require individual or group practice of some specific skill,
such as speech composition, problem solving procedures, weapon
effect computations, or operational planning . Most seminars, however, are devoted to activities of a problem-solving nature which
require the concurrent use of several specific skills. The facts and
conditions of a hypothetical military situation are set down. Con-
ferees are asked to assume command and staff roles as members of
a concrete group; they are required to produce the best solution
or group consensus that they can reach in these roles.

This emphasis upon group work accounts in part for the early
instruction in semantics, logical thinking and problem solving, group
processes and group dynamics, human relations, and in the four
basic skills of speaking, writing, reading, and listening. Formal
lecture instruction is kept at a minimum. The stress is on individual performance. After the lectures, a series of exercises is arranged which require individual performance and receive individual
criticism. A brief review of instruction in the four basic skills may
be helpful.

Speaking. Each officer prepares six assigned talks and presents
them to the other students in his seminars. These speeches are
informative or persuasive in purpose and from five to 20 minutes
in length. We make every effort to construct realistic assignments.
In general, these assignments specify a staff speaking situation but
permit the student to choose and adapt his subject to fit that situation. The faculty adviser criticizes each speech, pointing out
strengths and weaknesses in composition and delivery and recom-
mending corrective measures. This "formal" speech program is
supplemented by a current-events briefing program. This is, during the first five minutes of each daily seminar one student gives
a briefing on a newsworthy item, or, if he wishes, the officer may
speak on a subject related to the seminar which follows. These

daily briefings afford each student several additional experiences in thinking and speaking on his feet.

Writing. We use a similar approach to the problem of teaching students to write. Students are assigned seven writing assignments, ranging from the simple to the complex — from writing a memorandum to writing a research paper. Again, these exercises are representative of the writing tasks which confront commanders and staff officers. The main purpose of the instruction is to provide an understanding of what we choose to call "readable writing" — simple, clear, direct expression of idea — and, by means of several writing assignments, to provide the student with an evaluation of how well he has learned the lesson. We suggest that the faculty evaluate student papers for meaning and clarity rather than give undue attention to grammar and mechanics.

Reading. Our reading instruction consists of two phases: professional reading and reading improvement. We try to motivate the student to further develop himself professionally through broad reading. Such books as *Power and Policy,* by Thomas K. Finletter, and *Strategy for the West,* by Sir John Slessor, are read and then discussed in the seminars. In the latter months of school, students are required to read and evaluate current books by military and civilian authors during certain units of instruction. These student book reviews are used by Air University Research Studies Institute to establish reading lists for inclusion in Air Force Pamphlet 34-11-1, *An Air Force Reading Guide.*

For a number of years we have also offered a Reading Improvement Laboratory on a voluntary basis to all students and faculty. The laboratory provides two programs of instruction designed to improve the reading speed, comprehension, and adaptability of our students. One program offers 20 hours of training for officers taking short courses, such as the Squadron Officer School and the Academic Instructor School. Officers in the Command and Staff College and permanent personnel are urged to take a 36-hour course. In addition, each student receives a pre-test, a lecture on the reading process, a one-hour orientation lesson, and a post-test.

Our primary training instruments are the ophthalmograph and the reading rate controller. During the first 12-14 hours of the course, the emphasis is upon developing speed and improving the mechanical habits of reading. The student becomes aware of the

limitations of regression and subvocalization, and he is encouraged
to develop a smooth, rhythmical sweep of the eyes with wide and
unvocalized fixations. During periods 14-20, instruction in depth
and speed of comprehension is increasingly stressed, and the exercises increase steadily in difficulty. During periods 20-36 the student is encouraged by instruction and in choice of material to vary
and adapt his speed and comprehension to the difficulty level of
the material.

We use the Harvard University Reading Course Tests A, B,
and C to determine the results of the training. Students consistently average a 60 percent increase in speed with a slight increase in comprehension — about five percent. Although we are
anxious to retest students to determine how well they retain their
increased proficiency, the only information to date comes from
chance interviews with officers who completed the course in past
years. Most of these men report a permanent change in their reading and study habits and substantial retention of their new skills.

Listening. On the first day of formal instruction, all students take the Brown-Carlsen Listening Comprehension Test. The
purpose is primarily motivational, and the test is immediately followed by a one-hour lecture on the art of listening. As part of the
speech program, students are often asked to turn in a "Listener
Report" in which they identify the speaker's purpose, main ideas,
and organizational pattern. The Command and Staff College
lecture program, which constitutes about one-third of the total
curriculum time, also provides an informal listening laboratory.
A portion of the student body — about 40 officers — evaluates
each lecture and submits individual critiques. These critiques require the student to re-structure the lecture and to identify main
ideas, as well as to judge the value of the instruction. Although
the primary purpose of the critique is to aid the instructor, it also
gives the student valuable practice in developing good listening
habits.

III

Because of the large student body and the lack of professionally trained instructors, each faculty adviser in these Air University schools and colleges must serve as a critic or teacher of communication skills. Despite obvious limitations imposed by using
non-specialist instructors, we feel that this practice has certain ad-

vantages. When the student sees that the entire faculty is sensitive to the need for effective communication, he may more clearly grasp the role of communication in military management than he would if the program were handled solely by a few specialists. Not only in formally assigned speeches and papers, but also in all school programs and exercises, the student's ability to express himself logically and clearly is evaluated. Thus we hope that emphasis on effective communication permeates the entire school to a greater extent than it might otherwise do.

All newly assigned faculty members are required to attend the 6-week Academic Instructor School. In addition, we work closely with them in workshops and other in-service teacher training periods to help them become competent critics and teachers. In sessions lasting from two hours to two weeks we teach methods for criticizing a group discussion, a piece of writing, or an oral presentation. We often observe their critiques and, in turn, "critique the critiquer." We prepare "faculty folders" containing guidelines for the instructor to use in evaluating each assignment or seminar project. In followup, we visit individual instructors and offer further help when help is needed. In other words, we do all that we can do to insure that all instructors are reasonably competent in our area of responsibility and that all are working toward the same objectives.

In general, then, our instruction is aimed at the goal of proficiency in thinking, speaking, writing, reading, and listening. We do not anticipate major changes in content, scope, or method of instruction in the foreseeable future. Even though we are working with adults who have been through the American school system — the majority are college graduates — their present need for improved communicative skill is likely to continue. Since human lives may pay the price for ineffectual leadership, the Air Force considers communicative ability absolutely vital in its commanders and staff officers.

chapter 21

THE FOURTH CLASS ENGLISH COURSE AT THE UNITED STATES MILITARY ACADEMY

*Colonel George R. Stephens**

I. *Mission*

The mission of the United States Military Academy at West Point, New York, is "to instruct and train the Corps of Cadets so that each graduate will have the qualities and attributes essential to his progressive and continuing development throughout a lifetime career as an officer in the Regular Army."[1] Certainly there can be no exact enumeration, even in very general terms, of the essential "qualities" and "attributes" which the Army officer needs today and will need in the future. But we know that the Army officer must have a broad general education in both the arts and sciences to allow him to function successfully in modern society in peace and in war. Thus, although the West Point graduate is awarded a Bachelor of Science degree, the "course of study cannot be classed as either liberal arts or engineering but has somewhat the character of both . . . . The course of study is designed to prepare the graduate for the diverse intellectual problems that confront an officer during his career."[2]

The Department of English plays an increasingly important role in this preparation. It is self-evident that no progress is possible in any professional field without a consummate knowledge and facile utilization of one's native tongue. The mission of the

---

*Head, Department of English.

[1]*Army Regulation 350-5*, Paragraph 25, 14 May 1952.

[2]*United States Military Academy Catalogue* (Washington: United States Government Printing Office, 1958), p. 45.

Department of English, therefore, is twofold: (1) to teach the cadets how to organize and express their ideas clearly and effectively in writing and speaking, and (2) to help cadets acquire a knowledge of the world's great literature so that they will be capable of enlightened leadership.   Inherent in our mission is the objective of assisting each cadet to develop his own philosophy of life.   The English Department believes, in the words of Sir Richard Livingstone, that ". . . the most important task of education is to bring home to the student the greatest of all problems — the problem of living — and to give him some guidance in it.   Nations and individuals are ultimately judged by the values and standards by which they are ruled."[3]

II.   *The Present Fourth Class (Freshman) English Course*

The objectives of the Fourth Class English Course are to teach cadets to think logically and to express themselves clearly and forcefully.   This course of 106 attendances — taken by all Fourth Classmen except for the top 8-10%, who are given advanced work — is subdivided into a writing course and a speaking course.   There is no reading course as such; but reading assignments are interspersed with the lessons on writing and speaking to afford material for the cadets' written work, speeches, and classroom discussions.

Cadets attend classes in small sections of about twelve to fifteen students.   Merit sectioning is used in English, as well as in all other courses.   The atmosphere in class is one of quiet informality.   Many of the periods are spent in discussion, and all cadets are encouraged to participate freely in the exchange of ideas about the various topics under consideration.   These topics include writing techniques and problems; speech critiques; and ideas presented in provocative essays on current problems.   The cadets also read two Shakespearean plays, several sonnets, Stephen Vincent Benét's *John Brown's Body,* and modern short stories.   The discussions of literary works are designed to challenge the cadets' views on various social, moral, and ethical problems.   The cadets are required to analyze carefully the issues involved, to formulate answers or solutions in light of their own experience, and to present these solutions for critical evaluation by their instructor and their classmates.

---

[3]Sir Richard Livingstone, *Some Thoughts on University Education* (London: Cambridge University Press, 1948), p. 21.

In this way, the "problem of living" is explored, and the cadets are expected to begin the formulation of their own philosophy of life.

The core of the Fourth Class English program, however, is expository writing; and the basis of instruction is critical discussion of cadet work. During the year the cadets write six paragraphs, thirteen themes, a précis, a book review, a feature article, an educational sketch, a process paper, and a research paper. From their reading, cadets select subjects about which they have a conviction; their problem then is to explain their attitude with such clarity and force as to convince their instructor and their classmates. During discussions of cadet work, the instructor reviews such fundamentals of writing as diction, sentence structure, paragraph development, and theme organization. The effectivness of the writing, however, is judged principally upon the cadets' grasp of the basic concepts of unity, coherence, and emphasis, and upon the soundness of their analysis and logic.

Most of the speech work is given early in the course, not as a block of lessons, but as a series of short speeches spaced a few weeks apart. The first speech is a four-minute speech to inform; later, the cadets also deliver a six-minute speech to inform and a six-minute speech to convince, as well as a five-minute special report. Both the class and the instructor analyze and critique each speech on the basis of subject matter, organization, and delivery. In addition, the oral participation of cadets in classroom discussions is carefully evaluated and graded. Generally, the same fundamental principles of unity, coherence, emphasis, analysis, and logic are stressed as in the writing course.

Comprehensive examinations are given by the department at the end of the fall semester and again at the end of the spring semester. The examinations are designed to evaluate the cadets' mastery of the principles of writing and speaking covered during each semester. Most of the examination requirements are short paragraphs or themes which test the same skills as those stressed during the semester.

In summary, the Fourth Class English Course is designed to give the cadets a basic foundation in writing and speaking. In addition, through critical discussions of various literary works, cadets are given an insight into the world around them which will assist them in developing their own philosophy of life.

As mentioned earlier, some 8-10% of the Fourth Classmen, those who have demonstrated exceptional ability, are excused from the regular course just described. These cadets take a special course in the dramatic evolution of American ideals in which they identify and trace certain prominent ideals revealed in selected American literature from 1607 to the present. The amount of writing remains approximately equal to that of the regular course but the specific assignments require several major research projects rather than a large number of short themes. In addition, panel discussions and other speech assignments supplement classroom discussions and lectures. The basic objectives of this course are the same as for the regular course: logical thinking and clear, forceful self-expression.

III. *Proposed Experimental Shifts in the Fourth Class English Course*

The members of the Department of English foresee no radical change in the department's basic mission and objectives. Some modifications of the present course, however, will probably be necessary. Among these modifications are (1) an increase in the present logic course to broaden its scope; (2) a shift of emphasis in the reading topics from the present essays and other literary works to a more detailed analysis of modern problems; (3) a re-arrangement of the time allotted to the Fourth Class Course: one semester at the beginning of each of the cadet's first two years at West Point; (4) an expansion of the special course in American ideals to two full semesters; and (5) perhaps the scheduling of electives for those cadets who have mastered the subject matter of the regular course.

At present, the Fourth Class English Course includes eight attendances devoted to discussions and practical work in logic. The impact of mass communications and propaganda and the present state of world affairs make it mandatory that the Army officer be well armed with the tools necessary for critical analysis and evaluation of ideas presented to him and of ideas which he himself may formulate. The department anticipates giving more emphasis to the logical analysis of the complex arguments involved in modern problems, and to a fuller understanding of the logical foundations of the cadets' own written and oral presentations.

In this same connection, the department feels that there should be greater emphasis placed upon understanding the broader issues in the world today. Certainly none of our students are English majors; cadets do not specialize in any one field. Thus, to stimulate interest and to prepare the cadets more adequately for "the problem of living," more emphasis should be placed on their understanding of the modern world and of the problems and tensions with which they must live.

Another change which will probably be instituted is a reapportionment of the hours which the cadets spend with the Department of English. At present, they have 106 attendances of one hour each in their Fourth Class (Freshman) English Course, 63 in their Third Class (Sophomore) English Course, and 27 in their First Class (Senior) Course. At present, Second Classmen (Juniors) have no course with the Department of English. It would be desirable to have the cadets have some contact with the Department of English in each of their four years to serve as a constant challenge to them and as a reminder of the vital importance of clear communication. At least one semester each year would probably provide the best solution. Under such a system, the first term of the Fourth Class year would be devoted to the fundamentals of writing, speech, and logic; the second term of Third Class year would consist of developing the skills acquired and of introducing the cadets to modern problems as a foundation for the literature course to follow; the first term of Second Class year would comprise a study of the literature of Western civilization and its application to modern problems; and the second term of First Class year would complete the cadets' study of English by stressing modern literature and modern problems. This reapportionment would not necessitate any change in the department's mission or any increase in the total number of hours devoted to the study of English. But it would give a balanced program which would be much more effective in accomplishing the objectives of the department.

Another experimental shift which may be instituted in the near future is an expansion of the special course in American ideals previously discussed. This course at present is taught in the second semester of Fourth Class year. The validity of modern testing techniques is such that it should be possible to identify the superior students earlier in the year. Under the proposed four-year program just discussed, these students would begin the special course in the first semester of the Fourth Class year and complete it in the second semester of the Third Class year.   At the end of the first half of the course, those students who have failed to meet the special-course requirements would revert to the regular English course.   On the other hand, those students who have done outstanding work in the regular course could be integrated into the special course for the second half.   Clear, logical, forceful self-expression would remain as the primary objective of the special course.

The unique mission of the United States Military Academy has led many to argue that electives are inappropriate at West Point because all cadets are being prepared for careers in the Army.   But an ever-increasing number of graduates are now going on to postgraduate training in many diverse fields in numerous civilian colleges and universities.   Consequently, those cadets who have mastered certain phases of the basic curriculum should be allowed to specialize to some extent in a major field of interest.   Specifically, in the Department of English, it would be beneficial for those Fourth Classmen who have a solid foundation in the fundamentals of writing and speaking to do advanced work in some area of communication such as linguistics or semantics.

IV.   *The Communication Course at West Point in 1970*

Probably by 1970, the shifts discussed in Section III of this paper will have all been instituted.   The communication course will likely consist of one semester of about forty-five attendances each year for the first two years, with electives available for those cadets who qualify.   In 1970 it will be increasingly necessary that basic communication be emphasized.   Certainly in the technological civilization in which we shall live, communication among the various specialized fields will be increasingly difficult.   The Army officer of 1970, if he is to function successfully, must be able to deal with the physicist, the chemist, the biologist, the historian, the economist, the jurist, and a host of other specialists.   Therefore, West Point will devote more and more effort to developing the generalist who can understand the problems of, and communicate with, all of these specialists.

But in 1970, the basic mission and objectives of the department will probably remain unchanged.   The department will still seek to teach clear, logical, effective oral and written self-expression and will still seek to help the cadets to acquire a knowledge of the world's great literature so that they will be capable of enlightened leadership. Enlightened leaders in all walks of life, moreover, are the men who have developed appropriate philosophies of life to serve as guides in the conduct of their day-to-day affairs. The Department of English recognizes its obligation to give cadets such a philosophy of life as well as to train them in basic communicative skills.

chapter 22

THE ART OF READING AND WRITING AT VASSAR COLLEGE

*Caroline Mercer**

I. *Rationale, Materials and Methods*

Our fundamental principles in the teaching of English to freshmen are two.   One is that the individual student is the center of the course: we try to begin at the point she has reached in her ability to understand and enjoy literature and to use language, and help her develop further power.   This principle is expressed in the fact that each of our twenty-one sections follows its own plan, devised for that particular group, and that considerable freedom is given to individual students within each plan.   We have two courses, with separate designations: "English 105, The Art of Reading and Writing: Contemporary Literature," and "English 130, The Art of Reading and Writing: Periods of English Literature." The instructors of both are free, within the framework of the courses, to choose their materials and to a considerable extent their methods.   (We assume that it is well for the instructor to choose material which he can teach with zest.)   The second principle, which determines the general framework, is that freshman English is taught as an introduction to an art and not primarily as a means to proficiency in the use of a tool (although we wish to extend whatever technical skills our students have learned in the schools). These are not courses from which students are to be exempted; they are not required, although about 95% of the freshmen usually elect them.   Some of our students are ignorant or ill-trained but our

---

*Professor of English.

problems of illiteracy are smaller than those of many institutions. And the faculty believes that teachers of all subjects share the responsibility for training students to read, speak, write, and use the materials of scholarship.

In introducing students to the art of English at the college level, we seek to help them achieve vitality in thought, feeling and expression, and a precision learned from experiment rather than from the application of rules. This is not an encouragement to mere adolescent self-expression: our object is genuineness, not egotism. We use reading and writing together, as elements of an art that derives its significance from human experience and in turn enlarges and illuminates it by giving it form. Thus reading and writing are joined not simply as model and copy or even theory and practice, but as related events in a human activity large enough to include the young writer: an activity that involves writers, readers, the world they know or can learn about, and the sense or form they can make of it.

"Freshmen," as one of our instructors recently said, "are interested in the whole world; sophomores like to discuss technique." And yet we find that, without organizing the courses around types of literature, we can study a few kinds of design in literary composition and bring a freshman to see that the form of a work — her own or another's — is part of its meaning. We hope to free our students from the rigidity of form in composition and from the pretentiousness in language that some of them bring with them. We expect our ablest and best prepared students (and many are very well prepared) to begin to write with considerable control and subtlety and to notice subtle uses of language in what they read.

All instructors assign approximately one short paper a week, hold six or more conferences a year with each student,[1] and bring many of the papers to the class for discussion. The class discussion — as lively and cogent as we can make it — is a very important part of the course, for it is here that students speak and listen, learn how a group can put together and enlarge the thoughts

---

[1]The sections are of from 17 to 20 students; they meet three times a week, with a fourth scheduled hour which can be used for class meetings, group meetings, or extra work by the students. The usual teaching load in the department is three courses, usually three different courses, with a total of from 45 to 60 students. We have no lecture courses.

of its members, and perceive that experiences of various sorts can be brought to bear upon literature.[2]

We eschew study hints and warn students away from reading analyses of works being discussed or written about, asking them to read for themselves, however naively, and to subject their findings to the test of class discussion. We all, however, use critical essays that can be studied as works of art, used to illuminate other works, or offered as stimuli for thought — from *The Poetics* to James Baldwin's *Notes of A Native Son*. Finding and evaluating source materials is part of the training. Most of us make use of "raw" materials — documentary, social, historical, biographical — in order to assist imaginative understanding of a work by placing it in a social context, to provide study of how form has been made from raw experience, or to set before students their own problem of making imaginative order from unformed matter.

These are methods commonly used. But we have no syllabi and no set texts.[3] The teachers of the courses meet informally to discuss problems and exchange useful discoveries. Sections are taught by members of the department of all ranks, in fact by almost every one every year. (We have no Assistants.) And the courses are universally regarded as challenging to a teacher. The choice of material, especially, presents interesting problems. The teacher must find assignments that will relate themselves to existing interests and yet open up new concerns and take the students beyond their present stage of imaginative perception. He must avoid seeming to repeat work done in secondary school.[4] And he must devise his own ways of giving freedom in assignments without confusing the students, of making use of extra work done by the energetic, and of propelling every one quietly toward some kind of independence.

---

[2]We do not section students on the basis of ability as we did in the past, when our range was wider than at present. We see advantages in variety: as a whole group, for example, can learn much from a gifted student, and she in turn can extend her power by listening to people who, although less polished as writers, may view matters with a freshness and concreteness which she lacks.

[3]Students buy inexpensive editions of the central texts, and use the library for other materials. The library is open-shelf, and in addition has open reserve shelves where intensively used materials can be kept.

[4]In September the students report on their work in school. The teacher, in consultation with the class, frames the first assignments and makes a rough plan for the year, usually much modified as he goes along. He will of course use his past experience and to a considerable extent guide the students: they cannot make a course plan.

English 130 (usually given in six or seven sections) is not a survey of English literature or even of its major works; it moves towards our common ends by means of material chosen from three or four periods, not necessarily in chronological order, although care is taken to suggest the intimate connection between a work and its historical context.   (We urge students to elect if possible also a course in European history and one in French literature so as to help them understand the culture of the past.)   The students try to discover what made a piece of literature "contemporary" in its day and what makes it interesting today.   Emphasis is upon careful study of a few works, and upon constant writing.   A section might begin, for example, with a paper in which each student was asked to describe some aspect of life intimately known to her, the object being to put before the class the kinds of background against which the older literature would be read.   It might — like many sections — read a few literary essays raising questions about changing tastes and other relevant matters.   It might proceed to study "The Man of Law's Tale" so as to see Chaucer writing a story set in an older time, perhaps together with a modern narrative looking back to the past.   It could then go back to the past behind Chaucer, with *Beowulf* and some of the Saints' legends and Christian poetry.   Another class, beginning with a play of Shakespeare, might follow its themes back to the Middle Ages, moving say from *Othello* to "The Clerk's Tale" and "The Wife of Bath," and thence to "The Knight's Tale" and *Gawain and the Green Knight*.   Both classes would have some short critical papers, some free assignments (permitting students to write poetry) and some papers calling upon them to consider men and manners in their own day, and they might have occasion to write a short narrative of their own.   Longer critical papers usually come later in the year, when students have had experience with sources of information about older periods and training in the unaided analysis of difficult material.   So, for example, upon arriving at *Samson Agonistes,* a class might also study *Murder in the Cathedral* and write papers upon Becket in history and legend and Eliot's use of the figure, to put beside Milton's use of a hero from the Bible.

English 105 (usually offered in fourteen or fifteen sections) does not attempt to give a history of modern literature, but uses modern materials for its purposes, drawing upon older writings as needed.   A class that was to read *The Waste Land,* for example, might begin with a careful study of several Greek plays; another class might study Jefferson's *Notes on Virginia* with Oppenheimer's *Science and the Common Understanding*. The problem of putting together reading and varied writing assignments is of course more easily solved in English 105 than in English 130. Thus one class recently began with *The Lonely Crowd* and wrote two papers, one saying what their home locale would look like to a stranger, the other discussing the "parental role" as they had known it. Their criticisms of Riesman's language led them to a study of essays on language and to papers (choosing their own materials and form) upon language in advertising. They discussed poems about non-conformity by Cummings and Marianne Moore, and studied a volume of Mencken's *Prejudices*. The last papers in this section of the work were a discussion of a point raised in one of the books criticizing American life which they had read from a list of suggestions, and a free paper, in which many took up something in Mencken.

Another class took off from the students' interest in a speech at the opening convocation on education in a world of violence. They read Yeats' "A Prayer for My Daughter" by way of contrast, and then an excellent memoir by one of our graduates from the Orient, describing her youth in wartime. They read *Journey to a War* and some of Auden's poems (he was to be at the college very shortly) and with these *The Dog Beneath the Skin* and parts of Spender's *World Within World* and of Sevareid's *Not So Wild A Dream*. Papers included an account, in any form, of a personal experience of shock or violence, and a paper suggested by a journey (several students had been to Russia, and one to Japan on the American Field Service plan). Their next "composition" was a set of research notes to be used in a class discussion of what is happening to students and intellectuals in Communist China. At the suggestion of one of the students, they discussed Chester Bowles' *Ideas, People, and Peace,* which brought up questions about structure in a political essay, differences between responsible and irresponsible uses of language for propaganda, and connections between literary imagination and political action. The class was then divided for two weeks into four groups, one consisting of the most interested writers, the others of people who wished to engage in reading projects growing out of the discussions. The rest of the year took them into closer analysis of language and form in fiction and poetry, and finally to a discussion of essays in science and ethics, including Russell's *Why I am Not a Christian*, and Freud's *Introductory Lectures in Psychoanalysis*, with Auden's "In Memory of Sigmund Freud." The teacher had planned to make Trilling's *Freud and the Crisis of Our Culture* the focus of the concluding papers and discussions, but the students seized upon another text assigned, Oppenheimer's *Knowledge and the Structure of Culture* (a transcript of a lecture that they had attended in the autumn) and discussed it thoroughly in the light of their other courses and the year's work in English. The final paper was a free assignment which resulted in a great variety: attempts at scientific essays, a comparison based upon Planck's *Scientific Autobiography*, of the scientific and the literary kinds of imagination, a satire on the narratives in "Beat" magazines, essays on personal beliefs, a characterization of the quality of Einstein's mind as a layman can see it in his writings, and several poems.

II.   *Current Experiments*

In a sense every instructor constantly experiments. As a group we are discussing how best to meet the changes due to new programs in the schools. Because we attempt to begin with all students' needs and because we conceive that most freshmen, even the unusually gifted, can profit from a course that takes advantage of their being at a freshman's stage of experience, we have not wished to institute an extensive program of Advanced Placement. Recognizing, however, that an occasional freshman might be best educated in a sophomore course, we have announced that as a limited experiment we will consider recommendations for the admission of freshmen to intermediate courses from independent and public schools, whether or not the students come out of courses designated as preparing for Advanced Placement. We have so placed a few students. We are also discussing our various ways of educating the ablest students, and in 1959-60 plan to select a small group of the best writers from all sections to work for about a fourth of their time in the second term with a distinguished novelist who is to be on the staff.

III.   *The character of the course in 1970?*

This we cannot predict. Although our students, being women, will presumably not neglect the humanities, we may have to think freshly about the relationships of our teaching to the sciences and social sciences. It seems probable that our group will continue to read books, but we shall perhaps need to devise new ways to combat the vulgarity and corruptions of language to which every one is exposed. The students may need to study more explicitly ways to communicate with one's fellow citizens within the mass culture and yet be responsibly critical of it.

We speculate about the effect upon us of new courses in the secondary schools. (Our students, incidentally, come in about equal numbers from public and independent schools.) If they should increasingly assign esoteric works of literature in all languages, we may have increasing difficulty in freeing the students from literary jargon and the abstractions which are the result of reading works beyond one's comprehension. If teachers in the schools come to have lighter loads and be able to prepare their students in writing better than they do now, we shall be happy to try to carry their students still farther. As one of our professors remarked in a discussion some thirty years ago, "No one ever writes and speaks well enough."

chapter 23

THE BASIC COURSES IN ENGLISH AT WAYNE STATE UNIVERSITY

*Lester W. Cameron**

There are three different ways in which an entering student at Wayne State University may begin his college English. If he has enrolled in the general education program of the new Monteith College he will have no formal English classes but will expect to have all his instructors evaluate whatever he writes for its English as well as for its content. If he has enrolled in the Pilot Program, which is an experiment of the College of Education in cooperation with the College of Liberal Arts, he will have no formal English classes the first two semesters, but the papers written in non-English courses will be criticized by experienced teachers of English with whom the student will confer. These two ways of beginning college English involve only a minority of the students entering Wayne. Neither one was planned by the Department of English, but the department has cooperated by lending experienced members to both projects. Monteith College is in its first year, the Pilot Program in its second. The majority of freshmen, however, are, like their predecessors, under the direct supervision of the Department of English and take the sequence of three basic courses required of all except students in Engineering and Pharmacy, who need take only two semesters. What follows in this description has to do only with the departmental sequence of the basic courses, which was inaugurated in 1956 and which has been only slightly revised since that date. Only someone involved in the experiments would

---

*Chairman, Basic Courses Curriculum Committee.

be qualified to discuss in detail the program of Monteith College or the College of Education Pilot Project.

Before 1956 the departmental basic sequence of courses was composed of one semester of writing from experience, one semester of writing about abstract ideas, and one semester of literature, a reading course in which ordinarily only four critical papers were written. For reading the first semester, the department used its own anthology of material, *Writing from Observation*, now in its third edition, which shows how writers have used their powers of observation to write about subjects familiar to our students. For the second semester the reading was a collection of essays. The third semester reading was by types, the short story, the novel, the play, and the lyric poem.

The new sequence of courses, inaugurated in 1956, was based on the desire to more nearly equate reading and writing, to spread both more evenly over the whole three-semester sequence, and to have the students read more significant works of literature and to read them whole. The three courses are differentiated, according to their objectives, by the kinds of reading. The first semester presents narratives, the second the exposition of ideas as embodied in works of various types, and the third drama and poetry. To quote from the syllabus of the first course, "The intention of the basic courses is to promote in students the knowledge, understanding, and appreciation of literature which should belong to every college-educated person, and the ability to write English as they will need to write it in other university courses and in later business or professional life. Language as a medium of art and of communication is the link which connects the two activities."

In choosing the reading for the sequence the idea was to give some sense of the sweep of western culture, to include works of outstanding literary quality, and to show some of the basic ideas running through our literature; for example, man and society. The original choice for the first semester was a book of short novels, parts of the Bible, the *Odyssey, Huckleberry Finn,* and *Crime and Punishment.* Since then, a book of short stories has replaced the short novels, and the Bible, which some instructors feel incompetent to teach, has been made optional. For the second semester some of the dialogues of Plato, *Gulliver's Travels,* Thoreau's *Walden,* Shaw's *Saint Joan,* and Huxley's *Brave New World* are what remain after the reading list originally set up proved to be impossibly long. For the third semester, there are an anthology of plays from the Greeks through T. S. Eliot, a volume of Shakespeare plays, and an anthology of British and American verse.

The amount of writing is a minimum of about eight themes, class and outside, for each semester. They are expository in nature and vary in length from 500 to 1500 words. There are two library themes in the second semester; the themes of the third semester tend to be literary criticism of the works read in the course. The instructor meets his students in conference several times each semester. Proficiency in both reading and writing determines the student's grade.

The students are introduced to the university library by two talks. One, given in the first semester, is a guided tour to acquaint them with the geography and resources of the collections. The second, in the next semester, is timed to coincide with their work in the research paper and is designed to make them more specifically aware of the principal sources of information and the use and location of bibliographies. The library provides the staff for these talks and they are given to each class section separately. Instruction in the use of the dictionary is the responsibility of the instructor during the first semester; every student is required to have an acceptable dictionary.

The basic courses are run by a six-man committee appointed by the chairman of the department. The chairman of the basic courses is considered to have nearly a full-time job; he teaches only one course in addition to his administrative duties. The staff of the basic courses includes the whole department since there is a rule that every member of the department shall teach at least one section of the basic courses every two years. A considerable number of sections are taught by graduate fellows and assistants, but the bulk of the instruction is in the hands of the instructors, whose teaching load is three sections at the present time.

At present there is no experimentation in the department. We consider our present courses new and untested and want to appraise them carefully after sufficient experience with them before making any radical changes. The syllabi are being revised one by one but merely with the object of making them better instruments of the stated objectives of the present courses. The revision of the first semester syllabus was the work of the basic courses committee itself; it is now being tried for the first time this semester.

The basic idea of the revised syllabus is a division of the fifteen-week course into three parts: one of four weeks, one of five, and one of six. The first period is devoted to reading; the only writing, and this is optional with the instructor, is an occasional paragraph based on the reading. The student thus is introduced easily to the course. As much as possible, emphasis is placed on the linguistic aspects of literature, on the expression of ideas and the form of the works read rather than on the extraction of ideas.

The second part of the course, five weeks in length, involves the writing of at least one expository theme a week. The only reading done is the *Odyssey*, which is not discussed formally in class. In this period the emphasis is still on language, but now on the student's solution of the problem of expression rather than on the solutions of the authors he has been reading. Problems of correctness, effectiveness, and style and most of the formal remedial work, if the instructor finds that necessary, will be taken up in this period.

The final part of the course, six weeks in length, involves reading, rereading, and writing. The *Odyssey* has been read during the earlier period with the idea that the student can be taught the rewards of reading a work of merit more than once. Then the novel *Crime and Punishment* (and portions of the Bible if the instructor chooses to include that) are read. There are three themes, one, the longest of the semester, of 750-1000 words. All writing in the basic courses is exposition of one kind or another.

This approach to the teaching of reading and writing, which allows a concentration on writing after the student has been stimulated by concentration on reading, is the extent of experimentation at the present time. The recommended bibliography for instructors which is part of the syllabus is largely composed of key works of structural linguistics and freshman texts which have a structural orientation, but these do not serve as content in the course. The instructor can use structural linguistics or traditional grammar as he chooses to solve the language difficulties of his students but there is no part of the semester devoted to the systematic study of either linguistics or traditional grammar. However, it was the feeling of the committee that those of the staff who were uninformed about the latest scholarship in language ought to acquaint themselves with it. The staff is large and there is such a diversity of ideas on this matter that the department has not been able to find a handbook which is acceptable to all, and the policy of the basic courses is to allow as much individual freedom as possible within the limits of a course which must realize the same objective for hundreds of students each semester. It is always explicitly stated that the experienced instructor is free to consider a syllabus as a statement of the objectives of the course rather than as a plan of operation to which he must adhere closely.

Such is the state of the instruction in the basic courses at present at Wayne State University. There is no radical experimentation but there is the characteristic constant examination of what we are doing which prevents the courses from ever becoming static.